Recognising Asperger's Syndrome (Autism Spectrum Disorder) – Access your online resources

Recognising Asperger's Syndrome (Autism Spectrum Disorder) is accompanied by a number of printable online materials, designed to ensure this resource best supports your professional needs.

Activate your resources in three simple steps:

- Go to www.speechmark.net then create account / login
- Once registered, go to My Resources, where you'll be asked to enter the below activation code
- Once activated, all online resources that accompany Recognising Asperger's Syndrome (Autism Spectrum Disorder) will appear in the My Resources section of your account – every time you log in

ACTIVATION CODE* –

rjsdvhojia

id: 97

*Note, activation codes may be used on a one time only basis.

A number of new Speechmark titles are accompanied by supporting materials, accessible online. Each time you purchase one, enter your unique activation code (typically found on the inside front cover of the resource) and enjoy access to My Resources – your very own online library of printable, practical resources that may be accessed again and again.

Recognising Asperger's Syndrome

(Autism Spectrum Disorder)

A PRACTICAL GUIDE TO ADULT DIAGNOSIS AND BEYOND

TREVOR POWELL

Speechmark

Dedication

To the children and their children: David, Marita, Tanya, Jonathan, Sarah, Hannah and little Sebastian

First published in 2015 by
Speechmark Publishing Ltd,
2nd Floor, 5 Thomas More Square, London E1W 1YW, UK
Tel: +44 (0)845 034 4610; Fax: +44 (0)845 034 4649
www.speechmark.net

Design and artwork by Moo Creative (Luton)

002-6000/Printed in the United Kingdom by CMP (uk) Ltd

British Library Cataloguing in Publication Data
A catalogue record for this book is available from the British Library

ISBN 9781909301528

Contents

Preface

Everybody is a genius. But if you judge a fish by its ability to climb a tree it will live its whole life believing that it is stupid.

– Albert Einstein

This book is full of people's stories, words, quotations and struggles; I feel very much like a messenger. I have tried to capture the experiences of the clients that I have seen in our adult Asperger's syndrome (AS)/autism diagnostic and support clinic. The book is deliberately aimed at a broad audience of people: those who have just received a diagnosis and want to know more, those who are considering seeking a diagnosis, family members, relatives, friends and clinicians including mental health workers, psychologists, support workers and all those who work with people with AS. A final category is the wider general public. Learning about aspects of autism can tell us a great deal about ourselves and our own human nature.

A major difficulty writing the book has been the issue of language and labels: whether to use the term 'autism', Asperger's syndrome, autistic spectrum disorder (ASD), autistic spectrum condition (ASC), 'on the autism spectrum', 'people with autism' or 'autistic people'! The choices are numerous and all refer to the same condition. The autism community is in a state of flux with changes recorded in *The Diagnostic and Statistical Manual of Mental Disorders* (DSM-5), in which the global category ASD replaced all subtypes including AS in 2013. There is the question of whether 'it's all one condition and let's call everybody autistic', or whether to 'split' people with a higher level of independent functioning from those lower down the autistic scale. I am aware that the issue of using the term 'higher' and 'lower', or 'milder' is also controversial to some people. The use of language is a sensitive one – like walking through a minefield. This book is actually written for people with what used to be called Asperger's syndrome, and higher functioning autism, whom I will refer to as people with AS. But those initials are synonymous and could just as well refer to autism spectrum – it's all the same, there is no hard-edged difference. I will also use the term 'neurotypical' to refer to non-autistic people.

People on the autism spectrum are a very diverse group whose characteristics vary enormously, so not all the information in this book will be applicable to everyone. So, people with a diagnosis of AS will read parts of the book and are likely to say, 'I'm not like that'.

I came across people with AS in the late years of my career having previously worked in mental health, brain injury and neuropsychology. It strikes me that the adult autistic community is not unlike the head injury community 25 years ago – falling between the cracks of statutory provision, not really mental health or physical health – a lost tribe. It has offered me the opportunity and privilege to meet a refreshing, honest, fascinating, likeable and touching group of people. It has also given me a new lease of life and interest for which I am grateful.

written for people with what used to be called Asperger's syndrome, and higher functioning autism, whom I will refer to as people with AS. But those initials are synonymous and could just as well refer to autism spectrum – it's all the same, there is no hard-edged difference. I will also use the term 'neurotypical' to refer to non-autistic people.

People on the autism spectrum are a very diverse group whose characteristics vary enormously, so not all the information in this book will be applicable to everyone. So, people with a diagnosis of AS will read parts of the book and are likely to say, 'I'm not like that'.

I came across people with AS in the late years of my career having previously worked in mental health, brain injury and neuropsychology. It strikes me that the adult autistic community is not unlike the head injury community 25 years ago – falling between the cracks of statutory provision, not really mental health or physical health – a lost tribe. It has offered me the opportunity and privilege to meet a refreshing, honest, fascinating, likeable and touching group of people. It has also given me a new lease of life and interest for which I am grateful.

Acknowledgements

I would like to thank all the clients with AS I have seen in my work over the past decade or so. Their stories have been fascinating and heart-warming and are the bedrock of this book – the 'golden nuggets'. Their words and quotations have been anonymised in the main text apart from those who have specifically written pieces for the book in chapter 4: Katie, Joanne, Rachel, Jennie, Floyd, David, Melanie, Max, Charles and Julie. Thanks also to people with AS who have commented on my writing: Caroline and Tina. A special thanks to my colleague Ann Wilson, whose encouragement, insights and collaboration have been invaluable. Thanks also to other colleagues including Jessica Howse, Marjolein van Deurzen, Helen Harris, Georgie Boothroyd, Bhisma Chakrabarti, Anne Jeavons, Andrew Salter and Andrew Bates. Thanks also to Professor Simon Baron-Cohen for permission to use the AQ50 and Tony Attwood and David LeBlond for the poem. My thanks are due to Berkshire Healthcare NHS Foundation Trust, my employers, too for their support over the years. Finally, special thanks to my wife Meriel, who has given me longstanding encouragement and inspiration.

Chapter One

Considering a diagnosis of Asperger's syndrome

1 Four people's stories: Who comes for a diagnostic assessment?

Jenny sat opposite me in my consulting room, a single woman in her forties, who worked as an accountant. Her face was rather expressionless, and her eyes flickered between myself and the carpet. Rather directly, before I had finished introducing myself, she said: 'I think I've got a type of autistic brain. I want you to write a report to say I've got Asperger's syndrome, so I can tell my mother it's not my fault.'

Jenny had seen a programme on television about AS, had researched the condition extensively and felt that it explained her lifelong difficulties. She had come to me for confirmation. She told a story of her difficult relationship with her now elderly mother:

> On one occasion when I was about six years old, my mother who was pregnant with my younger sister said to me in a temper, 'If this baby is anything like you I don't want it'. That has always stuck in my mind. I know I was a difficult child, but what I want to know is was I awkward or did I have autism?

Jenny gave an insightful description of how her brain worked:

> I have a brain that is attracted to detail. I love reconciling things – I don't care if it's a balance of one million pounds; I need to get it right down to the last penny. I am extremely organised and am a systematiser. My DVDs are organised alphabetically; my books are sorted by author; and my clothes are organised by type and colour – although most of my tops are grey or navy and my trousers are black. My kitchen cupboards are sorted by food type, such as Italian, Chinese, Indian, baking, sauces and tins.

However, when talking about her social life she commented:

> I have a small number of friends but I find meeting people is like going to the dentist – a necessity. I can never think of what to say and am never

> sure when it's my turn to talk. I always try and avoid the firm's Christmas party and on the odd occasion I have gone I've felt exhausted and ill afterwards.

Another incident narrated from Jenny's childhood provided further insight into her social difficulties. She told me:

> I must have been about five or six years old and I was happily playing with my Lego and stuffed animal collection on my own when my mother suggested I should go and play in the sandpit with other children. I said to my mother: 'I don't know what they're doing. I don't know the rules. I'd rather stay in and play on my own.' I remember her being angry with me and calling me 'awkward Annie'.

Her mother could not understand her and always thought she was being deliberately difficult as she would only eat certain foods, didn't like being picked up or cuddled and had to have things in a particular way; otherwise she would throw tantrums.

Stuart was 22 years old, with long blond hair in a ponytail, and was accompanied by both parents, who were sitting either side of him during the assessment interview. His mother said: 'I've told him he can't spend the rest of his life in his bedroom. All he does is play on that computer, sleep and eat.'

Stuart mumbled, 'I'm OK, I'm happy, why don't you just leave me alone?'. The referral had come from a psychiatrist who had diagnosed Stuart with depression, agoraphobia and social phobia. Stuart had left school with good A-level results – A grades in Physics and Maths. He had started a course at university on 'Designing Multi-person Computer Games', but had dropped out at the end of the first year. The academic work had not been a problem, but Stuart had become increasingly isolated, finding social situations really stressful. He had said to a fellow student on the first day of the term: 'I am an introverted introvert. I do not find social situations invigorating like most people but draining … don't take it personally.' After returning home to the warm love of his parents and the cocoon of his bedroom, Stuart had become more avoidant and more isolated. He would not catch a bus on his own and wouldn't answer the doorbell or the house phone.

As a child Stuart had been bullied and teased at school because he was different. The other children would find his detailed and pedantic way of explaining things amusing and would tease him in the playground just to 'set him off'. Stuart was like 'a little professor' and got on better with people older than his peers, being happy to sit and play a board game with adults. His father said, 'He never attempted anything unless he was 110 per cent sure he could do it, including walking, swimming and talking – everything has to be precise and just right.' I was told that Stuart as an infant had started to walk very suddenly, in a very 'all or nothing' manner, as there was not much crawling or tottering. His parents reported that this 'all or nothing manner' was further illustrated by him deciding and telling his parents, 'I'm not wearing a nappy anymore, I don't need to.' Stuart was bored at preschool because he wanted to do his sums and didn't want to play with the other children or draw, and he had learned his alphabet before he went to school. He commented:

> I was looking forward to going to school because I thought I'd get an education. But on the first day we spent most of the time colouring. I thought, this is ridiculous and felt disappointed and frustrated. I was more advanced compared to the other children and would go around the class helping them to speed the lessons up. Towards the end of the infant school they took me out of the class and left me in the library with all the books and said 'Get on with it'. That was great for me because I could study paleontology and dinosaurs.

Stuart had been diagnosed by the psychiatrist with social phobia, but careful questioning revealed what was underneath that anxiety. Stuart explained: 'My anxiety is created by random events … I need to have things planned; I want a degree of certainty; I'm afraid that if I don't know what is coming, I'll do something wrong; I'll create a problem; I won't know how to cope.' When Stuart dropped out of university, he planned to design his own computer games but soon realised that he needed to work as part of a team as he couldn't do it on his own. When I finally diagnosed Stuart as having AS, it meant that he had a recognised 'hidden disability' and was entitled to some extra help and for others to make reasonable allowances. Stuart's reaction to getting a diagnosis was a mixture of anger and relief. He said: 'If the incidence of Asperger's is one in a hundred why does it have to be me? But I suppose I am relieved to know ... it will take me a time to process, as I tend to keep my feelings in a box.'

Lara was a 40-year-old woman who had been arrested and charged with attempted bodily harm and assaulting a police officer. The duty court solicitor, who had a nephew with AS, thought Lara might be 'on the spectrum' and requested a diagnostic assessment. Lara was unemployed and lived with her parents. Every Tuesday morning, after cooking her breakfast, carrying a lunch box which always had exactly the same items in, she would catch the 09.45 train to London, on her own, to visit the Natural History and Science Museums. She enjoyed examining the exhibits and making her own catalogue. Lara found the journey stressful as she didn't really like travelling on the underground, but she coped because she had a set routine and stuck with it. One day there was a closure on the underground and Lara had to take a different tube. The underground was very crowded, and people were funneled, shoulder to shoulder, barging and shoving down a narrow concourse. Lara's anxiety, already high due to her change of routine, became extreme because of the noise, the crowds and the people touching her. 'Please don't touch me', she shouted out to a man pushing into the back of her. The man ignored her. 'Don't touch me, stop it', Lara shouted. She then turned and hit the man with a rolled-up newspaper, and a scuffle ensued. Lara tried to run away when they reached the concourse, but her assailant grabbed her in front of a transport policeman. The policeman tried to separate them, but Lara lashed out again punching the police officer. Lara was arrested and put in a cell. She commented: 'I couldn't help it. I was completely overwhelmed, with the noise, the lights, the crowds, being touched, and the change in my routine and had a complete meltdown.' The man Lara had hit said that he would drop the charge if she apologised and admitted that she was in the wrong. But Lara was adamant that she wasn't in the wrong, as she had only hit the man to defend herself after telling him twice to stop pushing and touching her. The man hadn't heeded her warning. She could have apologised and walked away with a caution, but Lara had a very rigid set of beliefs about what was right or wrong and found it difficult to accept the view of others. Lara was later diagnosed with AS, and the accompanying report explaining her hidden disabilities allowed the judge to dismiss the case.

Jack was a 40-year-old IT specialist – a systems architect – who came, with his wife, a social worker, for an assessment. He had come because he was having difficulties with his manager at work and was involved in a disciplinary hearing. Their son Oliver had been recently diagnosed with autism, and both his wife and the diagnosing pediatrician thought Jack might have the condition too. Jack commented about his son's diagnosis, 'I don't really think there is anything wrong with him – he's just like I was as a child.' Jack described his childhood when he enjoyed lining up his Thomas the Tank Engine models in terms of length, colour and which were his favourites. Jack said, 'My life was transformed with the introduction of the Spectrum ZX computer.' He said that at college he was rather isolated having only one friend and had no idea how to get a girlfriend. His wife, Sarah, commented: 'I noticed him, but he was hopeless and had absolutely no idea that I liked him even though I was giving him all the signs, like always saving him a seat next to me at the Halls of Residence dining room – I had to do all the running.' Jack commented: 'Yes, Sarah has been a lifesaver for me. I would have literally been lost without her. She helps me with most aspects of my life.' Sarah commented about their marriage: 'I love him because he is unusual, fascinating, but very, very honest and loyal even though he has an awkward disposition. There is no bullshit with Jack, but there is also not much overt affection.' Jack had recently had problems at work communicating with his manager and on a number of occasions hadn't completed tasks he'd been asked to do. Sarah commented:

> Jack just doesn't understand what his manager wants; it's as though they both speak a different language, at cross purpose, which means the meetings they have are enormously frustrating. He needs very specific instructions–nothing vague. He might lose his job. I saw a sign outside in the clinic reception saying 'interpreter available' and thought 'yes that is what Jack needs when he speaks to his boss, someone to translate and explain what each is saying to the other'.

2 What is Asperger's syndrome?

All these four individuals have one thing in common: a late diagnosis of the condition. As adults, their struggles in life led them each eventually to the late diagnosis of AS, which is a milder form of autism. Getting a diagnosis helped each of them in different ways: Jenny found greater peace with herself; Stuart received a more appropriate psychiatric diagnosis and got more tailored help; Lara avoided going to court; Jack managed to keep his job. AS is a type of autism which is hidden, which is why it had not been identified earlier in those four people's lives. To all intents and purposes, the person appears perfectly normal, often very intelligent, living relatively independently, with near-typical language skills, but under the surface there are a number of subtle hidden disabilities. These four people – Jenny, Stuart, Lara and Jack – are on the higher end of the autism spectrum, or scale, that is, they function relatively independently, while at the lower end is 'classic autism', a more disabling condition.

I have a clear memory of having worked with a man called Lucas, many years ago, who had classic autism. Lucas had below-average IQ, with little speech, and an array of repetitive stereotyped behaviours such as rocking, insisting on eating the same food and repetitively watching the same DVDs of *Thomas the Tank Engine and Mr Bean.* He lived in a residential care home, dependent on a team of support workers for many self-care needs. He rarely made eye contact but, when he went to the supermarket with his carers, had a tendency to stand very close to strangers and stare at them inappropriately. He had no particular friends apart from the care staff who looked after him, had never worked or had a girlfriend. Lucas liked mechanical toys like Meccano and particularly liked taking televisions apart and reassembling them. In certain circumstances he got very stressed and had what the staff referred to as a 'meltdown' when he would shriek and bite his hand.

What have our four case studies and Lucas got in common? They are considered to be lying on the same underlying autism spectrum or continuum – illustrating how broad and diverse that spectrum is. All have difficulties in communication and dealing with the social and emotional world, accompanied by unusually strong, narrow interests and repetitive behaviours. However, it could be argued that their differences are greater than their similarities. This is the debate that rages within the world of autism and AS, between the 'lumpers', who say, 'it's all the same and we'll call it autism', or 'ASD' and 'splitters' who say, 'people at the higher end of the spectrum with Asperger's are very different and should be in a separate category'. There are arguments for both sides. Until recently there was a clear division in diagnostic classification between people at the higher, less disabled end of the spectrum, who had a diagnosis such as

Asperger's syndrome or high functioning autism, and those people below-average conventional intelligence, with more severe language and communication difficulties, called autism. The recent American diagnostic classification, the DSM-5, has simplified its diagnostic categories and reduced four subtypes of autism into one condition named autism spectrum disorder or ASD, getting rid of the widely used popular name Asperger's syndrome (AS) and the less widely used label of 'high functioning autism'.

A colleague of mine once worked in a school for people with AS who were all very bright and often progressed to tertiary-level education. Five miles down the road was a special school for pupils with autism, most of whom had a learning disability. The Asperger pupils saw themselves as very different from the pupils in the autism school and did not like mixing. I recently attended a workshop on 'Communication Issues in Autism', by specialist, linguist and author Olga Bogdashina, who has a 27-year-old son with classic autism and a daughter with AS. She commented: 'I think it is a mistake for DSM-5 – my two children differ more from each other than their peers. My daughter speaks five languages and is at the university.'

The issue of labels is topical and contentious. Some people with AS feel disenfranchised by the changes in DSM-5, saying, 'we've lost our label and our identity'; others proudly say, 'I'm autistic and proud of it', and a few more say, 'I'm an Aspie and don't care what the official medical diagnostic classification says'. A recent online survey of more than three thousand people, led by the National Autistic Society (NAS), found that there was no single term that everybody preferred. All groups, which included people on the spectrum, families, friend and professionals, liked 'on the autism spectrum' and 'Asperger's syndrome' although professionals preferred ASD more than the other groups. Clinicians working in the area are waiting for the other major classification of health conditions, the World Health Organization's

ICD-10, to reach a verdict. However, the present situation presents a problem for any likely author of a book on the subject. This book is about, and for, people at the higher end of the autism spectrum in terms of independence – people with AS. The reclassification means that AS has become ASD, which is a term that I will occasionally use alongside 'autism', and 'on the autism spectrum'. The terms mean the same thing and any confusion is a reflection of our present understanding, or lack of understanding about the condition

DSM-5 suggests that ASD can be classified into three levels of severity, depending on the level of support required. Officially the people I see in my clinic can be diagnosed ASD Level One, and add in brackets (Asperger's syndrome). This condition is characterised by persistent deficits in two dimensions: (1) social communication and social interaction and (2) restrictive, repetitive patterns of behaviour, interests or activities. To get a feel of the condition I will describe the most common traits in each dimension. Bear in mind that a person does not have to have all those traits to obtain a diagnosis.

(a) Social and communication difficulties

- Difficulty with a range of non-verbal behaviours such as eye contact, facial expression, voice intonation and gestures that are normally used to regulate normal communication.
- Difficulty reading and interpreting other people's non-verbal behaviours such as reading the emotion and intention in other people's facial expression.
- General lack of interest in other people – preferring to be alone. Struggling to develop and maintain friendships, peer relationships and romantic relationships.
- Difficulty having a two-way reciprocal – backwards and forwards – conversation, making small talk or chit-chat, or sharing information about self appropriately.

- Not understanding the unwritten 'social rules' that people generally pick up naturally, and sometimes behaving in a manner that is inappropriate, either being too direct, honest or blunt, not taking the feelings of others into account.
- Having a very literal interpretation of language, leading to the difficulty understanding nuances, jokes, sarcasm, metaphors and being rather pedantic.
- Difficulty knowing and expressing their own feelings, and difficulties anticipating or reading how somebody else might be feeling, which often presents as reduced feelings of empathy.
- Difficulty accepting that there may be other perspectives, not just a single rigid, correct perspective.

(b) Narrow interests and repetitive actions

- Having strong, narrow special interests or preoccupations that are often abnormal in intensity or focus, that often lead to great expertise in a particular area.
- Liking predictability, repetition, routine, sameness, order, rules and rituals – finding change and unpredictability stressful and upsetting.
- A good eye for detail, a good memory for facts, with the ability to focus on one subject intensely, but a difficulty pulling back, switching attention, multitasking and seeing the overall picture.
- Sensory issues such as disliking touch or particular textures, loud noises or certain tastes, smells or visual stimuli. Occasionally, under sensitivity to certain bodily states which might include hunger, temperature or tiredness. Having a tendency to be overwhelmed by senses.
- Poor coordination, clumsiness, poor body awareness and fine motor skills and possibly some stereotyped or repetitive motor mannerisms such as rocking, spinning, hand flapping or finger twisting.

3 A dash of autism and the rise of civilisation

From the list given earlier, it is apparent that an ASD can be a diverse cluster or a constellation of symptoms that co-occur. These can be both a strength, such as great concentration, specialist knowledge and intelligence, as well as a weakness or disability in the areas of understanding the social and emotional world or coping with the sensory world. Throughout history, people with autistic traits have led successful, celebrated lives in the sciences, arts, business and politics. Civilisation would not be where it is today without the influence of autistic thinking. Allan Snyder, director of Sydney University Centre for the Mind, commented, 'Nobel Prize–calibre geniuses often have certain core autistic features at their hearts'. Hans Asperger, after whom the condition was named, said, 'it seems that for success in science or art, a dash of autism is essential'. High achievers throughout history are thought to have had 'a dash of autism', including Albert Einstein, Charles Darwin, Isaac Newton, Hans Christian Andersen, Lewis Carroll, Thomas Jefferson, Wolfgang Amadeus Mozart, Andy Warhol, and Gregor Mendel. Who would have thought that Charles Darwin's boyhood fascination with bug-collecting would form the basis of the theory of evolution and tell us about our oneness with nature? Who would have thought that Albert Einstein, who did not speak until he was three, had no friends and rarely mixed with children his age, being described as the 'odd boy out', would go on to win the Nobel Prize and become the father of the theory of relativity? As a child he was introspective, avoided light conversation, but when something caught his interest he had 'the concentration of a watchmaker' and a 'laser-like ability to focus', according to those that have chronicled his life. He also had a 'lack of a tactful manner', a reputation for bizarre clothing choices and unconcern about his appearance – his uncombed hair a signature feature.

More contemporary figures include most of those people who were the founding fathers of computers, which have transformed our lives. One of the pioneers of the first computer was the British mathematician and code breaker Alan Turing, who undoubtedly had a 'dash of autism', as seen in the film *The Imitation Game*. Ashley Stanford wrote a fascinating book entitled *Business for Aspies* (2011) which shed insights into the development of the IT industry in California. She grew up in Silicon Valley in California, married a man with AS, who was an exceptionally talented coder and programmer and founded a successful IT company. She pointed out that numerous successful people are often not particularly 'well rounded' but have focused on their strengths. She comments on page 23:

> When you look at the top thousand most successful people of this generation you find a surprising number of them with Asperger traits. ... One of the richest men in the world was Bill Gates, a man known for having many obvious autistic traits. I grew up near Redmond where Bill Gates established the Microsoft Empire. Many of my friends and acquaintances worked for Gates in the early days of Microsoft's growth. The stories of his fits, rages, rocking, obsessing, stimming, flapping and irrational hold to logical structures were part of many conversations with friends.

Stanford points out that in her view of the four men who contributed most to building up computer operating systems in the world, three exhibited mild to moderate autistic traits. Those men were Linus Torvalds who developed the Linux operating system, Bill Gates who developed the Windows operating system and built the Microsoft Empire and Steve Jobs and Steve Wozniack who developed the Macintosh operating system and built the Apple organisation. Stanford suggests the only one who didn't have autistic traits was Steve Jobs. Autistic or 'black and white', logical, binary thinking and the ability to concentrate for lengthy periods and have an attention to detail are an obvious advantage in the field of computing.

Temple Grandin, one of the most famous and successful autistic/ Asperger people, has written books and lectured on autism, and is now professor at Colorado State university, is a living role model.

She writes how she had delayed speech as a child, was taunted for being different and was the weirdo at school whom the 'cool' kids teased. But she found a mentor in a science teacher at school who fed and encouraged her hunger for knowledge and understanding. Her natural affinity with animals, in particular, the cattle on her aunt's ranch, led her to becoming a successful animal behavioural specialist and designer of humane cattle-handling facilities. Over half the cattle in the US and Canada are handled in the humane chute systems she designed. There is now an Emmy Award-winning film about her life. She commented: 'After all, the really social people did not invent the first stone spear. It was probably invented by an Aspie who chipped away at rocks while the other people socialised around the campfire. Without autism traits we might still be living in caves.'

4 A brief history of Asperger's syndrome and autism

Examining the history of autism and AS sheds light on the complexity of the subject. Eighty years ago it was barely recognised, but now it has become the most talked about and controversial diagnoses of our time. The term Asperger's syndrome is named after the Viennese pediatrician Hans Asperger, who wrote an influential research paper in 1944. However, the word 'autism' originates from the Greek word for 'self' (*autos*) and was first used by the Swiss psychiatrist Eugene Blueler in 1912 to describe the thought patterns of schizophrenic patients and their difficulty connecting with other people.

Classic autism was first described by Leo Kanner, a child psychiatrist, in the US in 1943. He described autistic aloneness or profound lack of social engagement in 11 children who had a great difficulty appreciating another person's point of view and at the same time were very literal and experienced great difficulties with change. The first case was a boy called Donald T, who was described as being 'emotionally indifferent' and having an 'inability to relate', who had spent a year of his early life in an institution. Kanner referred to this syndrome as a form of childhood schizophrenia, saying that it was very rare and inadvertently caused by the parents because of their 'cold perfectionistic' parenting style.

At the same time in Europe, Hans Asperger, a pediatrician working in Vienna, made similar observations about a group of children, describing a milder form of the developmental disorder. Asperger described these children with autistic traits who had an IQ in the average range or above range and who frequently had very good attention and memory for detail, often being interested in acquiring unusual knowledge, wanting things to be done in the same way over and over again and being socially awkward or withdrawn. He referred to some of them as 'little professors', gifted, solitary, with precocious abilities and a fascination with rules, laws and schedules. Asperger, however, did not go on to point the finger of blame at the parents. Interestingly, Hans Asperger appears to have exhibited many of the features named after him as he was described as a 'remote and lonely child', who had difficulty making friends, was exceptionally good at languages and was particularly interested in an Austrian poet Franz Grillparzer, whom he used to quote to his uninterested and exasperated classmates. His landmark paper was clear in suggesting that he was under no illusion that the patients were budding geniuses and that, 'Unfortunately in the majority of cases the positive aspects of autism do not outweigh the negative ones.'

It was Kanner in the US who became famous, an autism celebrity, writing papers, and books and giving lectures. However, he made little or no reference to Hans Asperger, and did not cite his influential paper. Indeed Leo Kanner spoke German, so he could have read Asperger's paper without it having been translated and even worked with one of the old colleagues of Hans Asperger. The excellent book by Steve Silberman entitled *Neurotribes* (2015) traces the history of autism, uncovering Kanner's suppression of the truth. The baton for 'blaming the parents' and spreading Kanner's theory of toxic parenting was picked up by another celebrity psychiatrist called Bruno Bettelheim. Like Kanner, Bettelheim was a refugee from Europe – a concentration camp survivor – who emigrated to the US. One of the books he wrote was entitled *The Empty Fortress* (1967) in which he described autism as an illness, 'a suicide of the soul', and described the mothers as 'refrigerator mothers'. How damaging and unfair we now know this completely misguided belief to be and how awful for the parents to be associated with this type of shame and stigma! Not only did he blame the parents but suggested various therapies to attempt to rescue the child from this condition. These included hour after hour of psychoanalysis, or, worse still, different forms of holding therapies, where mothers were required to 'tame' their children by hugging them and starring into their eyes. Undoubtedly many lives were ruined by this cruel misunderstanding and pointing the finger of blame at parents.

Eventually this theory started to crumble, and the anti-psychiatric movement of the late 1960s and 1970s began to produce evidence that psychoanalytical treatments were often more harmful than beneficial. Leo Kanner, whose theories initially blamed the parents, was later to apologise, asking the parents to forgive him. Studies of autistic twins replaced the bad parenting theory with evidence that autism had complex genetic roots. Studies of parents of autistic children showed they were no less caring than other parents, and with the subsequent development of neuroscience we now know that people with autism have non-typical wiring of the brain. We also know that autism is primarily a genetic condition and that both parents contribute 'risk genes'.

Hans Asperger's landmark paper from 1944 was brought to a wider audience by the British psychiatrist Dr Lorna Wing in the 1980s. Lorna Wing had a daughter Susie, who had autism, and recognised how little support there was. She was the first person to translate Asperger's paper from German and give it wider prominence. She

significant psychological step which involves some degree of loss, grieving and adjustment.

(ii) Younger people in particular do not want to be considered different and might be reluctant to accept a diagnosis. The diagnostic assessment has to be handled with care, at the right time, and the person has to be ready for it; otherwise they are likely to feel stigmatised.

(iii) Relationships can change. People might view the person differently, making unhelpful assumptions. In marriage and families, feelings might change and in the work place there may be discrimination, and the individual may find it more difficult to get promotion or feel scrutinised.

6 Not needing a diagnosis

Many people who might be somewhere on the autism spectrum never receive a diagnosis. There is no clear dividing line between people with autistic traits, or so-called 'eccentrics', 'geeks', and 'boffins' and people diagnosed with AS. Tony Attwood (1998) describes this well: 'It is a seamless continuum that dissolves into the extreme end of the normal range ... there are people who have a "ghosting" or "shadow" of the condition' (p145). At their best level they might be considered eccentric or unusual: they might be mathematical geniuses, computer whiz kids or artists. At worst, they might be people who are isolated, function poorly and might be considered to be lost souls, who slip into the psychiatric services.

Many of us have neighbours, friends or people we know who might have clusters of traits. I have a friend who collects old motor scooters and has an extensive knowledge of technical detail relating to engines, cars and computers. When we have a conversation, he will launch into a topic with a lot of technical detail and I will have no idea or interest in what he is talking about, but he will seem quite oblivious to my lack of interest. I also have a social worker friend who mentioned he thought his younger sister had Asperger's. She had always lived at home with his parents, although she is now in her late forties, always carried out the same job in a library, always had the same sandwiches for lunch, had never had a boyfriend or many friends, and had little understanding of the complexities of social relationships. But she has an encyclopedic knowledge of films and visits the cinema twice a week on her own, always has a cooked breakfast on a Sunday and would never dream of having one on any other day – a creature of habit. Another friend has a son who as a child was suspected as having mild Asperger's but who never received a formal diagnosis. He was very rigid in his behaviour, insisting on having his food separated on a plate rather than mixed up and at school got into fights with the school bullies because he felt that what they were doing was wrong. He had certain sensory sensitivities: hated loud noises, the sound of a vacuum cleaner and smell of lilies. Now in his twenties, he has improved over the years; his social skills are better, although he still finds 'small talk' difficult, but does not see the benefit of having a label. A colleague commented about her ex-husband, who is a chief motor racing engineer, 'Gerry is definitely on the spectrum'. Amateur diagnosis of autism has become something of a trend, which hopefully doesn't trivialise the condition. However, I am sure we all know somebody who is 'on the spectrum'.

7 Improving over time – growing out of a diagnosis?

As we grow up, we all develop skills and learn ways to compensate for our weaknesses. This is true of people with AS, who may grow, change and grow out of some of their AS traits. A research study by Seltzer et al (2003) assessed 405 individuals who had met the diagnostic criteria for ASD as children, and found that among whom only 55 per cent met the criteria when re-examined as an adult. Another study by Patricia Howlin et al (2004) reported that 90 per cent of people with ASD show an improvement in ASD symptoms over the course of a lifetime and only 2 per cent get worse. She identified a decrease in problem repetitive ritualistic behaviour and an improvement in reciprocal social responses.

On the subject of change and diagnosis, two people described different experiences in our clinic: One man said: 'I have socially re-engineered myself. I have had life coaching, training in non-verbal communication, social skills, speech therapy, public speaking, psychological therapy etc. I am now different to what I was, but it's all just a veneer; scratch the surface and I am the same.' On the contrary, Jamie was 19 years old and wanted to join the army. He said: 'I can't get in the army with a diagnosis of Asperger's which I have had since I was six years old. I think I've grown out of it. I want you to remove my diagnosis. My eye contact is better. I'm better at small talk, I'm not so obsessed by things and I'm less rigid.' Jamie had indeed made progress with social skills, scoring just below the diagnostic criteria and left the assessment a happy man heading for a career in the army. Liane Holliday Willey, author of the bestselling book *Pretending to Be Normal* (1999, p133) said:

> Most of my AS traits continue to fade away but some don't, they hang in there tenaciously cropping up to trip me over ... Someone called it Residual Asperger's. I have improved, my eye contact is better, but eye contact still makes me nervous. Small talk is do-able but in truth it bores me to pieces and makes me anxious. I can deal with change pretty well, but I prefer no change.

8 Autism: A lens or mirror to view our own humanity

Many of the traits tail off into personality characteristics found in the general population which many people can identify with. Understanding these traits can help us to learn more about ourselves, like looking into a mirror or through a lens, allowing us to see ourselves more honestly, and raising questions about our own human nature. It is possible to get a rough idea of where we are with respect to the autism spectrum by considering the following simple questions.

- Do you feel more comfortable alone than with people?
- Do you like chit-chat or small talk?
- Do you feel comfortable expressing your feelings?
- Do you prefer predictable facts to more nebulous emotions?
- Do you like routine and predictability or change and variety?
- Do you hold very strong views and opinions?
- Do you react strongly to, feeling overwhelmed by, some sensory input?

I enjoy working with people with AS because they are often refreshingly different, straightforward and painfully honest – with little or no social pretension. They often see the world and think differently in a creative, fresh, unconventional and imaginative way – having thoughts that most of us take for granted. They are often vulnerable, struggling awkwardly to understand and negotiate the nuances of the social and emotional world we live in. People with AS are in some ways 'nonconformists', the ultimate 'anarchists'. They often don't obey the conventions, rules and norms concerned with celebrity, materialism and money, preferring comfort over fashion, work over play, hobbies over socialising. They often do their own thing and pursue their interests with a passion. Adults with AS have usually had a challenging time, and have the emotional scars that have resulted from struggling, surviving bullying and teasing and feeling isolated, marginalised and different. Working with people with AS teaches tolerance and understanding, acceptance and celebration of differences and diversity and compassion. It is about understanding human nature, both the head and the heart. It is about recognising that things don't always have to be perfect. Generally, people with AS do not rejoice over others' misfortunes. Life is not about greed, lust, gossip, competition or trying to get one over another person.

If everyone sticks to the rules, there is enough for everyone without competing or getting the better of someone. An ideal life is about having a routine, doing work, having a task to perform, information to organise, someone to love and a limited amount of socialising. This book is based on the knowledge I have gained from working with this diverse population of individuals, from both their perspective and my perspective. It is my hope that it will lead to improved understanding for both them and those who interact with them.

Chapter Two

Theories and facts about autism and Asperger's syndrome

1 What we know

We recognise that autism itself is a highly complex neurodevelopmental condition and that the causes too are complex and poorly understood. In this chapter we will look at what we know, including some of the facts and theories.

- It is a neurodevelopmental biogenetic condition, which means it is something a person is born with.
- People with autism have brains that are wired differently which affects the way information is processed in the brain.
- We know that autism is not caused by bad parenting; it is definitely not the parents' fault. Theories years ago around inadequate parenting were very damaging, misguided and misleading.
- It is a lifetime condition although people change and develop new skills and may move out of the diagnostic range. Talking about a 'cure' is not helpful.
- It is highly hereditary with strong genetic links and runs in families, but we do not know which particular genes are involved.
- It is a spectrum condition, so it is on a continuum or range from mild to severe. Some would argue that it tails off in its milder form into personality characteristics. It is not a straightforward spectrum, but one which has different constellations and many diverse forms.
- We don't really know much about what causes it, but we do know there is no link between the onset of autism and vaccination.
- Gender ratio: It is more common in males than females, although the estimated ratio has gone down from 10:1 to 3:1 in the past few decades.

There are various theories about autism which we will now consider.

2 Theory of mind

The theory of mind (ToM), sometimes referred to as 'mindreading' or 'mentalising', refers to a person's ability to recognise and understand the thoughts, beliefs, intentions, feelings and desires of others in order to make sense of their behaviour and predict what they are going to do next. Colloquially it means 'putting yourself in somebody else's shoes' or reading the intention of another. This involves taking a perspective other than your own. It also involves being able to reflect on your own thoughts and feelings – to stand back and look at yourself. The theory goes back to the seventeenth-century French philosopher Rene Descartes. If a person has difficulty taking the perspective of another, they are more likely to be puzzled by the action of others, have difficulty recognising and working out the feelings of others and are likely to find people unpredictable. If a person is not able to 'read' another person, they are more likely to encounter misunderstandings and have greater difficulties resolving conflicts. For example, they might wonder why someone is looking at somebody else in a particular way or why somebody spoke in a

Figure 2.1: Theory of mind

particular way. As a consequence of this they are also more likely to have lower levels of empathy, because they have difficulty picking up the cues that somebody might be upset. Without a good ToM life can be unpredictable and very scary.

Imagine this scene to illustrate the point. You are talking to somebody about your elderly father, who is ill and with whom you are very close. The other person starts blinking, looks down to the floor, their bottom lip quivers and they bring their hand to their face and wipe their finger across their eye. They are not openly sobbing or even crying, but there is a subtle change in their emotional state. We might interpret and attribute these cues and behaviour and their changed facial expression as signs that the person is upset or distressed. We might interpret that it has something to do with their father – maybe they had a close relationship and he has died, or maybe they had a poor relationship? We might ask if they are OK. We might predict that they might want to talk about it or not talk about it depending on the context. Their emotion might trigger emotion in us. All these things happen because we have a ToM which allows us to attribute, interpret and predict behaviour in others. People with AS might have more difficulty; they might struggle to pick up the initial change in facial expression as a sign of sadness; they might think that the person has something in the eye, rather than that they are wiping a tear. They might not link it to the emotional context of the conversation, or be able to judge whether the person wants to talk about it or subtly change the subject. People with AS may be puzzled by others and get anxious because they struggle to predict, interpret and anticipate what others are going to do.

Research suggests that most neurotypical children gradually develop this ToM, but for children on the autism spectrum there appears to be a time delay and poor subsequent development. At 14 months the child with autism has poor joint attention for carrying out tasks such as pointing and following another person's gaze. If a person points their finger at something, the child with autism will tend to look at the person's finger rather than what they are pointing at – failing to read the intention of the person pointing. At 24 months they struggle to engage in pretend play. At four years, various tests can be given to children to check whether they have developed the ability to take another person's point of view or perspective. The most famous of these is the Sally–Anne test. Children are introduced to the test as a story, usually presented as a series of cartoons, with two characters: Sally who has a basket and Anne who has a box. Sally has a marble and puts it in her basket, puts the lid on it and goes off for a walk. While she is away, Anne transfers the marble from Sally's basket to her box and puts the lid on that. Sally returns and the child is asked, where does Sally look for her marble? The autistic child is more likely to say Anne's box, because that's where we know it is. But Sally doesn't know that and if we put ourselves in her shoes she would look in her basket. The autistic child finds it difficult to look at the action from Sally's perspective. This is referred to as a false belief test.

At the age of nine, children with autism tend to fail a test called the faux pas test; this test suggests that children on the autism spectrum don't recognise what might hurt another person's feelings. Various research studies have examined young children with autism where they are shown animated films and cartoons and asked what happens next. The autistic children describe the physical aspects of the story, but are poor at describing the intentions or mental states of the characters. People on the autism spectrum are not as good as neurotypicals at interpreting expressions from somebody's eyes.

Underlying poor ToM is the theory that people on the autism spectrum have a one-channel, single, literal perspective of the world. One obvious consequence of a poor ToM is a very literal interpretation of what people say. For example, if somebody makes the comment 'Pull your socks up', meaning 'make more effort', the autistic child might literally start pulling their socks up. People with autism are not very good at 'reading between the lines' or interpreting those kinds of metaphors and are not very good at reading a person's intention unless they are spelt out very clearly and directly.

For most people with AS this collection of processes involved with understanding and relating to other people – known as ToM – is not completely absent, but is acquired later, more gradually and is often dormant or not used as much. Often if the person with AS is prompted, by being asked, 'what do you think they are thinking', they can answer reasonably well, but the problem is they don't do it spontaneously. It is almost as if the person with AS needs external cues or prompting, to 'hack' out the answers to understanding the mental states of others, it doesn't just happen naturally and spontaneously.

A further consequence is that people with AS are often remarkably honest and do not recognise that there is sometimes a need to tell 'a little white lie' to avoid causing offence or upsetting other people's feelings and generally smoothly oil the wheels of social interaction. One cause of this being brutally honest and blunt is the result of not being able to hold in mind how the other person might be feeling. This trait means that the AS person is often labelled as disrespectful and inconsiderate. Another consequence of literal one-track thinking is that people with AS often have a strong sense of social justice, or moral code, liking to keep strictly to the rules. This is an admirable quality but can sometimes get the person into trouble. Coupled with this, they have difficulty managing conflict, being poor at the art of persuasion and compromise and poor at understanding the perspectives of others. People on the autism spectrum often lack negotiating skills, tending to be more rigid and confrontational. They may have difficulties attending to someone else's agenda or sharing joint attention which can present as defiance.

Penny worked at a large local leisure centre as a sports officer, but ended up leaving her job after she became a 'whistle blower'. All this happened before she obtained her diagnosis. Penny comments:

> I enjoyed my job but was never any good at the 'banter' and could never pick up when people were joking or serious. I was also really upset by some of the practices of some of the older members of staff which included allowing friends and family to enrol their children free of charge on certain courses and on one occasion selling old equipment such as table tennis tables and not giving the money directly back to the council. I just couldn't let it go. I am the kind of person who always has to follow the rules and would never even walk on the grass if it said not to. I reported it to my manager, which created all sorts of problems as afterwards I was bullied and teased. I reported another member of staff for bullying and then it seemed all relationships got worse and most people were against me. I couldn't resolve all the conflicts and became really upset, depressed and eventually left.

Penny's difficulty reading people's intentions and understanding their perspectives, honesty, rigid moral code and difficulty managing conflict all contributed to her losing a job she loved.

3 Weak central coherence theory

This theory suggests that people with autism are remarkably good at attending to detail but appear to have considerable difficulty perceiving and understanding the overall picture or the gist. They focus on detail which results in a 'failure to weave together information to extract meaning'. It's as if the person is looking at the world through a rolled-up piece of paper or a pipe and can attend to things in detail but not step back and 'see the wood from the trees'. They can be fascinated by the swirls of their own fingerprints, get stuck in a groove, having difficulty shifting attention, having difficulty with change, multitasking and making new plans. This is sometimes referred to as a 'bottom-up' processing rather than 'top-down' processing, where the person starts with the details rather than the 'whole'.

Being able to ignore the bigger picture and focus on the details might in some circumstances be an advantage. For example, being very good at games such as 'Where's Wally' and picking out an embedded figure. People with AS see things in pieces not as wholes and when drawing something will often start with a secondary detail, not the general outline or might be pedantic in language often overemphasising a detail rather than summarising, or might see part of the face such as a worry line rather than seeing the whole face and picking out the emotion.

The autistic brain picks up too many details in everyday life, which might be an advantage in maths, coding and programming, copy editing, engineering and accountancy. But, in ordinary day-to-day life, the person with autism or AS is seeing every blade of grass, every branch of every tree, every cow in the field and it is not an advantage. Coupled with this overload of sensory details is the overload of the unpredictability of the social environment. It might

Figure 2.2: Theory of central coherence

be that the AS person's reaction to this overwhelming overload is to try to control and order, to systematise, break things down into categories, create structure, routine and rituals, so that the world becomes orderly and more predictable. This generates a sense of sameness, which feels safer.

Amanda was a 30-year-old lady whom I saw for a few sessions of psychological therapy after she obtained her diagnosis. She agreed to come to these sessions only if we had an agenda, or specific purpose, so she would know what was going to happen. The first session's theme was 'rigidity and flexibility' and after about half an hour, I inadvertently strayed off theme and we started talking about her artwork and art in general, which she found difficult. She commented:

> It's exhausting keeping track of everything people say – all the details and random conversations. For example, why don't you stay on track? You go off the rails; you're not sticking to the point. We are supposed to be talking about rigidity and now you're talking about art! I like to have structure, control and routine. I get stressed particularly easily if things change. I used to have to have everything straight and perfectly aligned, including my books, CDs and papers. I have to be precise and do things properly. I plan everything, make to-do lists and mini lists, have goals and objectives.

Interestingly, Amanda had quite severe sensory sensitivities and always removed the ticking clock from the consulting room before our session started. She hated certain smells such as scent and soap, disliked physical contact, buzzing lights, noisy electrical appliances, bright lights and shopping centres. It was almost as if she had to cling on to routine and structure because she was being bombarded with so many unpredictable small details –sensory, cognitive and social. It was as if she couldn't either filter out or ignore details or parcel them up into more manageable 'chunks'.

4 The extreme male brain theory – testosterone, empathising and systematising

Professor Simon Baron-Cohen (2008) suggests that the two key defining characteristics of autism are the skills of 'empathising' and 'systematising' and that these skills are opposite each other – the more empathy you have the less systematising you have. Empathising skills involve understanding the emotional and social world, being interested in others, responding to others with eye contact and gestures, being sensitive to the needs and feelings of others, recognising emotion and distress in others, feeling for the other and acting compassionately. In contrast, systematising is a drive to analyse, spot patterns, understand and construct systems and the rules that govern those systems, in order to predict how the system will behave. People, who are systematisers, ask questions and want to know how things work; they might collect information; they might be interested in mechanical systems (taking engines apart and reassembling them); they might study numerical systems such as timetables, geographical systems such as maps, make lists of capital cities, show intense interest in language systems being particularly involved with syntax, or musical systems which involve notations, or movement systems such as taekwondo. Systematisers prefer predictability, repeatable patterns and resist change. Being an above-average systematiser often explains why a person has narrow special interests, repetitive behaviour, resistance to change and the need for sameness. Systematisers like the truth, as put very simply, 'the truth' is a verifiable, repeatable pattern.

Baron Cohen's research indicates that there are clear sex differences between male and female brains and this is linked to the level of testosterone in the amniotic fluid in the mother's womb before the child is born. The more testosterone the more the brain tends towards that of being a classical male brain or 'systematiser' (liking to follow

Figure 2.3: Dr Simon Baron-Cohen

rules, being good at detail, liking to analyse), and the lower the level of testosterone, the more the brain tends towards being a good empathiser, a more classically female brain (having better social skills, more empathy and a better understanding of the emotional and social world). Research into babies' early reactions shows there are sex differences from the first day of life, where girls are more likely to look at faces and boys are more likely to look at mechanical mobiles. Males produce twice as much testosterone in their testes and adrenal glands and are therefore more likely to have these systematising autistic traits. In the very early months before the effect of socialisation the boys tend to prefer to play with toy vehicles such as cars and trains or construction toys like Lego, and girls tend to prefer to play with dolls. This is the same in monkeys. Higher foetal testosterone levels in childhood from 12, 24, 48, 96 months is consistently correlated with rated measures such as poor eye contact, poor social skills, poorer ability to read the emotion in the eye test, lower empathy and higher systematising and other autistic traits. The higher level of systematiser a person is, the lower they are at empathising. Generally, males score

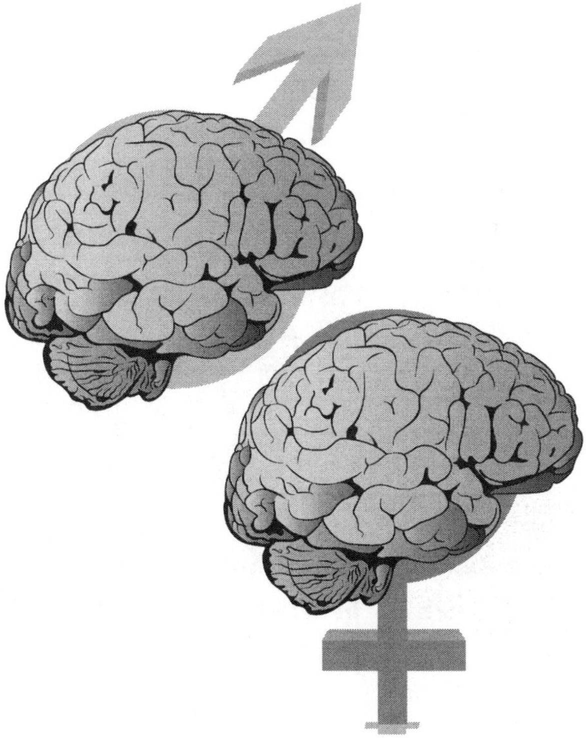

Figure 2.4: The extreme male brain theory

higher on systematising than females, and people with autism score higher than both average males and females on systematising and lower on empathising.

5 Autistic infants: Social rewards centre not working?

The British autism study of infant siblings researched babies, early infants and toddlers, and their hypothesis was that children with autism had an initial lack of attention or interest or sensitivity to social rewards or socially relevant information. Results suggested there was a reduced spontaneous ability to interact with others such as a lack of ability to respond to gaze cues or look at faces, to coo, babble, seek a cuddle, point, smile or make meaningful gestures. There is a lack of ability to engage in the give and take of everyday human interaction and to pay attention to the needs and feelings of others. There is also a difficulty in regulating emotions and a tendency to lose emotional control more readily. The lack of smiles and reinforcers from the baby produces a similar response in the caregiver – the lack of reciprocity reduces the caregiver's desire to interact with the child as they are not getting a response. Autistic children are slower to interpret what a smile, a wink or a grimace means – the social world is bewildering. This initial impairment precludes later development of key social and communication milestones such as joint or shared attention. The autistic brain is not targeted to look and scan the environment for human faces, and the reward centres in the brain do not light up automatically when they do lock on to a human face.

Various remediation therapies are evolving, such as 'Intensive Interaction', to help prevent the emergence of disabling consequences. These involve careful, often painstaking, tuned in stimulation and interaction, capturing the infants' attention, positioning face to face, at eye level, at a comfortable distance, encouraging the babies to respond to a smile. The therapist will deliberately and sensitively play 'peek-a-boo', or sing a nursery rhythm 'Incy wincey spider' to get a reaction. With hard work the therapist attempts to get the children to start smiling, so that the social engagement becomes intrinsically rewarding; they are then more likely to smile at another smiling face. The aim of the intervention is to try to activate and re- embroider that part of the brain where a smile is rewarding. There are some encouraging results from these types of interventions.

6 Compensatory strategies for being different

Tony Attwood (2007) suggests that there are four main ways a young child copes with feeling different from other children, which can mask diagnosis and make it more difficult to detect. This is part theory and part Tony Attwood's clinical observation. The idea is that in order to survive, the autistic child consciously or unconsciously might adopt one, or more than one, of these strategies. How the child compensates and what strategies they use depend on the child's personality, family, circumstances and experiences.

Strategy 1: Self-blame and depression: Those children who tend to internalise thoughts and feelings might become self-critical, blame themselves and become increasingly socially withdrawn. The child might desperately want to have friends but doesn't have the necessary social skills to do so and recognises that short fall. Low mood can lead to avoidance, lack of energy and have an adverse effect on sleep and eating.

Strategy 2: Escape into imagination: Some children escape into an alternative internal world of imagination and fantasy and even create imaginary friends. One client, Jessica, said: 'I didn't have any real friends and had an overwhelming desire to keep away from people apart from my family. I preferred the company of my imaginary friend Sarah and her brother James.' Escape can also lead to an interest in other worlds such as science fiction and fantasy or possibly an interest in astronomy or geography or another special interest. If that fantasy world becomes too extreme and the person becomes too detached from reality, they might be suspected of developing delusions.

Strategy 3: Imitation: A constructive compensatory strategy is to watch, observe, learn and imitate other children or characters in books, films or TV. Some children become remarkably good actors having the ability to mimic and copy other people. There is a veneer of social success but underneath the person may feel the same and still feel different as they are aware they are 'pretending'. However, some people become so accomplished at this pretence that they then have difficulty convincing others that they have real problems with social understanding and empathy. Some people even go on to develop a career as an actor.

Figure 2.5: Dr Tony Attwood

Strategy 4: Denial and arrogance: Children may develop a form of overcompensation for feeling inadequate in social situations by denying that there is a problem and pointing the finger of blame outwards at other people. They see themselves as 'above the rules' and have difficulty admitting to being wrong or making a mistake and often end up arguing their case very skilfully. They certainly would not want to be referred to an assessment team for a diagnostic assessment or might find it difficult to accept that they have AS. Sometimes they can become dominating and controlling in social situations, as a way of masking their own social difficulties.

7 Gender differences and the female presentation

The female presentation has been termed 'the invisible end of the spectrum' because girls often fly under the radar undetected. Girls seem to have a greater awareness of the need for social interaction and a greater desire to interact with others, often being perceived as 'just being shy' rather than a 'loner'. Their range of coping skills camouflage their difficulties as they are often good observers, being good at imitating, mimicking and emulating popular peers. They often have one or two good friendships and tend to be 'looked after' or protected in their peer group.

The linguistic ability of AS girls is often above average, and they tend to have better imaginary play abilities than males and can fantasise and escape into fiction and pretend play. However, there is a tendency in AS girls to be non-reciprocal, scripted and overly controlled. Imaginary friends are not uncommon with AS girls. Often the girl will be good academically, well behaved, following the rules, even top of the class, so will not alert the attention of teachers. They may read fiction books and watch soap operas as a source of information about the social and emotional world. Their restricted patterns of interests tend to involve people/animals rather than objects/things (eg animals, soap operas, celebrities, pop music, horses, fashion, pets and literature), which may be less recognised as related to autism. These special interests are noticeable because of their intensity rather than their focus. They also have a tendency to be perfectionistic, very determined and controlling. Their motor coordination problems are less conspicuous in the playground and they are less likely to develop conduct problems. Sometimes they will say, 'I get on better with boys because they are not so bitchy, but are more straightforward and don't have cliques'.

Males are more easily diagnosed with autism than females; however, their difficulties often 'leak out' in visible ways such as failing to understand socially appropriate boundaries or standing too close. It is important for those diagnosing AS not to focus on the surface behaviours but to ask probing questions and get underneath the camouflage. Females with AS are often misdiagnosed with conditions such as borderline personality disorder (BPD) and eating disorders. One female client said, 'the most common response I received when disclosing my diagnosis was, "you'd never know".'

8 Autism runs in families – the strong genetic link

Autism has a strong genetic component, and early twins studies showed that if one monozygotic twin is diagnosed with being on the autism spectrum the chance that the other twin will also get a diagnosis is 90 per cent. In 90 per cent of people diagnosed with being on the autism spectrum, at least one member of the extended family had a diagnosis or several members had high autistic traits – referred to as multiplex. Only 10 per cent are 'simplex', meaning one-offs in a family. We also know that traits of autism, where there is no clinical diagnosis, also run in families. Fred Volkmar's (1998) research reported that 46 per cent of first-degree relatives of children diagnosed with an ASD had similar autistic traits, although usually subclinical or autistic personality rather than having the syndrome or disorder. Simon Baron-Cohen (2007) carried out research which suggests that it is common to find a parent who worked as an engineer, accountant, physicist, mathematician or IT specialist.

If a child is on the autism spectrum, the risk that a sibling will have the same condition is between 2 and 14 per cent, which is about a 30 per cent increase over the general population's prevalence. In addition, research suggests there is a much higher presence of autistic traits in first-degree relatives, such as parents and siblings, than second- and third-degree relatives .

9 Autism prevalence rates

The prevalence rates of autism have changed quite dramatically over the past few decades. Around 40 years ago it was thought that autism was rare and the incidence was 1 in 2,500, whereas today incidence rates are considered to be 1 in 100, according to a survey carried out by Gillian Baird in 2006 (Baird et al 2006). However, in a more recent study in the US, rates were found to be up to

1 in 68 (Centre for Disease Control and Prevention, 2015). These figures are diagnosable cases and do not include many cases who have milder degrees of the condition that might be on the autistic spectrum. There is an increase in prevalence, but is this just due to better recognition and understanding? There is another explanation: 'associative mating', meaning that people who carry a risk gene for autism are more likely to meet and mate with other people who carry similar risk genes. Putting the two risk genes together might produce a child with autism; although both parents might not have diagnosable autism, they might have shadow traits. An article in *Wired* magazine (December 2001) noted the higher incidence of autism in places like Silicon Valley in California. This is an area where people with high systematising skills or attention to detail come together to work as IT specialists, programmers, coders and engineers. The article suggested that whereas the incidence in the general population was 1 per cent in certain areas it might be 10 per cent in others.

Two other research studies are of interest. There is evidence that if a child is born to a father over the age of 40, there is 6 times more likely probability that the child will have autism than if the father were under 30 (King et al, 2008). This has to do with an increased level of mutations in the father's germ cells (sperm) after the age of 40. There is no increased probability if the mother is over 40. A second strand of research indicates that 10 per cent of extremely premature babies test positive for autism (Kolevzon et al, 2007). This is thought to be due to the babies' brains being exposed to many stressors during a very critical stage of development.

10 The autistic brain

Modern neuroscience has generated much evidence that indicate atypical development and differences in the autistic brain's structure and functioning. Our understanding of autism has moved from it being 'all in the mind' to being 'all in the brain' – from psychiatry to neurology. However, probably because the autistic community is so diverse, and the brain is so complex, there has been no definitive identification of any 'biological marker' or specific aspect of the brain, which would be like a key opening the door enabling understanding of autism.

Increased brain growth when young: We know that there is an unusual pattern of brain growth in those with autism in the first 2–4 years in certain areas and that their brains are bigger and heavier. The normal course of events, in the neurotypical brain, is that within years 2–4 there is a process called 'synaptic pruning' or culling. Brain neurons and synapses are initially overconnected to their neighbours, and as the brain develops a process occurs where irrelevant connections are culled. This does not seem to happen so efficiently in the autistic brain. Researchers have looked at neural connectivity in the autistic brain and found that communication and speed of processing information between different areas of the brain may be different. There is evidence that autistic brains have an excess of relatively short neuronal fibres, surface white matter, linking areas that are close together, producing what is called 'local overconnectivity'. These short fibres, like short cables, can often mean that the person becomes very good at details. There are relatively fewer longer fibres, in the deeper white matter, or long distant cables, connecting distant parts of the brain, meaning that the person is poorer at perceiving the overall picture. This means that the different brain departments are less connected; regions are not talking to each other, or are 'out of synch'. The amount of information that goes to the executive or the frontal lobes, where concepts are formed, plans are made and the overall picture is perceived, from the more distant detail-orientated areas at the back of the brain, is relatively low. This fits in with the theory that people with autism are poorer at 'top-down' thinking and tend to be 'bottom-up' thinkers, starting with the details and then slowly building a picture.

Imagine, for example, the effect of one auditory or visual cortical neuron being overconnected to lots of others. The effect would be that any stimulus or sensory input would be amplified like sound coming out of a massive pair of speakers. This sensory amplification is one explanation of the sensory sensitivities that people with autism experience. A second effect of this synaptic pruning not taking place is that long-range connections from the back of the brain to the front don't occur. However, this growth spurt doesn't last long and by adolescence there is an accelerated rate of decline in size and by the age of 30 the autistic brain is the same volume as the non-autistic brain. Scientists are not sure exactly why this happens, but it is thought that there might be age-specific changes in gene expression, molecular, synaptic and circuit abnormalities.

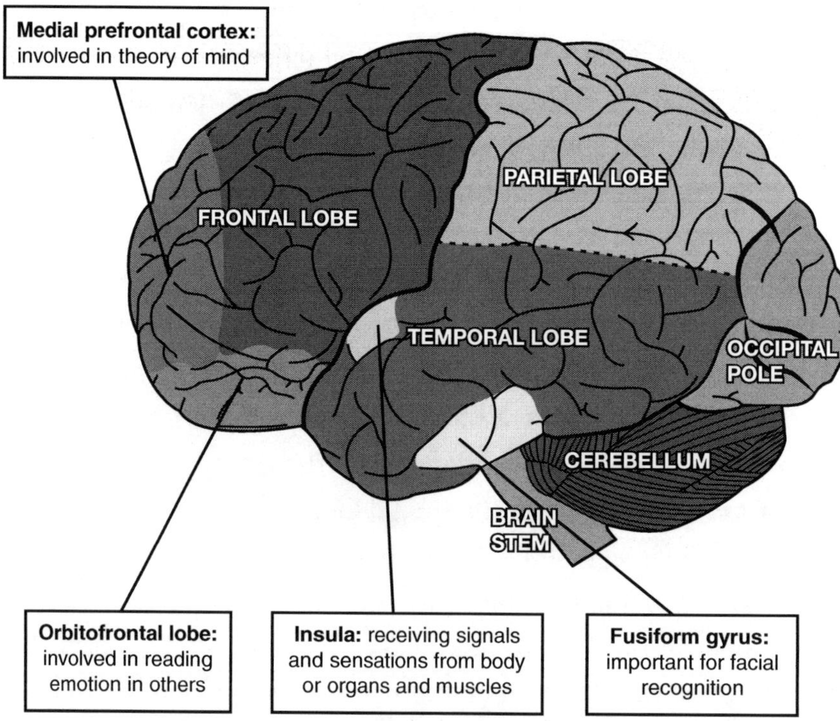

Figure 2.6: Lateral view of the brain and areas involved in autism

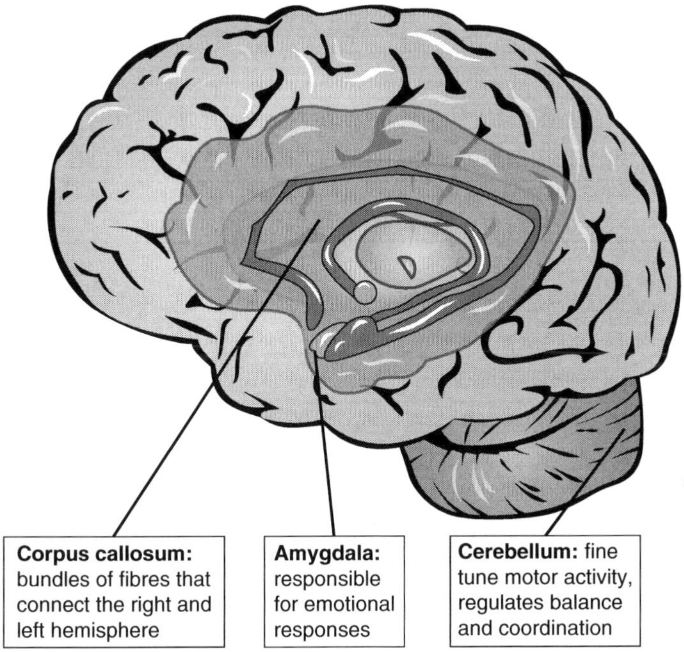

Figure 2.7: Medial view of the brain and areas associated with autism

Size of structures in the autistic brain: Neuroimaging studies have shown that various parts of the autistic brain are different from neurotypical brains. For example, a 2011 magnetic resonance imaging (MRI) study from the University of Louisville in the US compared a group of autistic people with non-autistic people and measured their corpus collosum – the band of thick fibre, like a bridge, that connects the right and left hemispheres. They found sections of the *corpus collosum were smaller* or differently shaped for most of the autistic group. The researchers could distinguish between the groups on the basis of the corpus collosum length with a level of accuracy of around 82–94 per cent. But, accuracy rates at that level are not quite high enough for researchers to say they have discovered a 'marker' for autism. However, a smaller corpus could explain limited connectivity among brain regions and help explain why people with autism have difficulty integrating complex ideas. There has been similar research showing people with autism have a *smaller cerebellum*, the walnut-like lump at the back of the brain that sits underneath the two hemispheres, behind the brain stem and is sometimes called the 'little brain'. Its main role is smoothing out movement, small motor coordination, balance and dexterity, timed movement, learning and reproducing sequences. A damaged or smaller cerebellum may explain why people with autism have poor coordination and tend to be clumsy. The cerebellum in autistic people has a reduced number of purkinje cells – the cells involved with motor coordination. A third area of note has been different *activity levels in the amygdala*. The amygdala is the almond-shaped structure buried deep in the brain in each hemisphere, which plays a significant role in generating and regulating emotional responses such as fear and desire. It is often thought of as the body's alarm system, the primitive brain, scanning the environment for danger. We know from functional MRI (fMRI) studies that the amygdala is frequently underactive in those with autism, particularly in tasks in which the person is trying to decode emotional facial expressions. However, other research indicates that there is overactivity when people with autism look specifically at somebody directly in the eyes (Dalton et al, 2005). The act of eye gaze activates the amygdala, creating anxiety and discomfort. When eye gaze is averted, activation of the amygdala falls, reducing anxiety. It is therefore understandable how this simple strategy of avoiding eye contact, to reduce arousal levels, can be learned and reinforced, and has a negative effect on non-verbal skills. The conclusion seems to be that responses of the amygdala are different in autism than controls but it depends on the type of stimuli.

Empathy circuits less connected: When people with autism are engaged in tasks involved with empathy or ToM (thinking about other people's thoughts, feelings, intentions or emotions), a network of brain regions, known as the 'social brain', is less active than in the neurotypical brain on fMRI scans. Like lights on a Christmas tree, if there are poor connections and one of these regions of the brain doesn't work, the whole network suffers. The main regions involved in this circuit include *the medial prefrontal cortex* – this area is in the middle of the frontal lobes. Some theorists say this area is necessary for a ToM – involved in the skills which compare one person's perspective to another person's and help us to understand our own thoughts and feelings. The *middle cingulate cortex* and the *anterior insula* are activated by pain, both when we feel our own pain and when we observe it in others, and are involved in bodily awareness. The *right temporal parietal junction* is involved in processing other people's actions – body perception, eye gaze – and helps us to judge another person's intentions and beliefs. The *amygdala* plays a central role in emotional learning and regulation.

Part of the problem is that research has focused on looking at this very diverse diagnostic group, where there is often large variability because people on the autism spectrum are different. If we look specifically at individuals' brains, it can be equally revealing. An example would be to look at *Temple Grandin's and Albert Einstein's* brains as they are unusual. Temple Grandin, possibly one of the most famous autistic people in the world, author and designer of humane cattle-handling facilities, has been involved in many studies of brain-imaging and has an intimate understanding of how her brain is different. She found out that her brain is not symmetrical and is 15 per cent larger than the control subjects'. Her cerebellum is 20 per cent smaller than the average, and as this area deals with motor coordination, it would explain why her lifetime sense of balance and hand–eye coordination is poor. Within the brain there are open spaces called ventricles and the chamber or ventricle on the left-hand side in Temple Grandin's brain was 57 per cent longer than the corresponding one on the right. The left ventricle is so long that it extends into her parietal cortex. She also found a neuroimaging study that revealed that the white fibre tracks that snake through her brain from the frontal areas to the areas at the back of the brain that deal with spatial and visual memory (occipital) were overconnected. In her words: 'I must have an internet trunk line, a direct line into the visual cortex to explain my visual memory. I thought I was being metaphorical but I realise at this point that the description was a close approximation of what was actually going on inside my head.' Temple Grandin says: 'My brain isn't broken; it just didn't grow properly. Hence I see the small detail before the big picture.'

There has been much speculation about the brain of Einstein, who was considered by many to have had AS, and arguably one of the most famous human brains. The story is that the doctor who carried out the autopsy removed Einstein's brain from his skull, unbeknown to his family, and stored it in two large jars in his office. Later, with the advent of more sophisticated technology, it was analysed and found to be smaller than the average brain weighing 1,230 grams rather than the average 1,400 grams – refuting the argument that the cleverer you are the bigger the brain. It was also found that the parietal lobes were unusually large, being 15 per cent wider than average brains. The left parietal lobe had an abundance of glial cells, outnumbering neurons by between 10 to 50 and 1. Since the parietal lobes are involved in visual and spatial computations, mathematical thought and the imagery of movement, this extra brain material in this area could explain Einstein's spatial and mathematical prowess. He said that he developed his theory of relativity by creating images and pictures of people on a moving train. Einstein is also known to have had delayed language skills; he was five or six years old before he developed speech. So his brain was likely to be weak on language and words but strong at visual and spatial perceptual tasks, which includes mathematics. A number of other famous and creative people had unusual brains. As a boy, Picasso struggled with reading, writing and arithmetic, but obviously had great spatial skills. Mozart had a savant-like or photographic memory for music and could remember note for note an entire symphony, on one hearing, without writing it.

Chapter Three

The diagnostic assessment

1 The diagnostic assessment – a jigsaw

Greater recognition of AS in adults has led to an increasing demand for diagnostic assessments. The diagnosis is based on an interview, observation of behaviour, tasks, questionnaires and the client's personal narrative. As yet there are no biological markers such as a blood test or brain scan. The length of the assessment varies considerably and usually takes anywhere between two and four hours but some clinicians might take all day. Often the assessment is carried out jointly by two clinicians. Where possible it is recommended to involve a family member, parent or older sibling, partner or other informant to provide collateral information, especially about early years. The diagnostic assessment interview is 'detective work' on the part of the assessor, trying to piece together the evidence. Tony Attwood (2007, p50), uses the metaphor of a jigsaw puzzle to explain the process.

> I explain to the client and family the concept of a 100 piece jigsaw puzzle. Some pieces of the puzzle (or characteristics of Asperger's syndrome) are essential: the corner pieces and the edge pieces. When more than 80 pieces are connected the puzzle is solved and the diagnosis confirmed. None of the characteristics are unique to Asperger's syndrome and a typical child and adult may have perhaps 10 to 20 pieces or characteristics. The person referred to a diagnostic assessment may have more pieces than occur in the typical population, but sometimes not enough, or the key or corner pieces, to complete the puzzle and receive a diagnosis of Asperger's syndrome.

The diagnostic process is not a precise science and is inherently problematic if we accept the idea that autistic traits lie on a spectrum or continuum. Again Tony Attwood (2007, p52) makes a valid point about where we draw the line.

> The final decision on where you draw the artificial line, namely whether a person has a diagnosis of Asperger's syndrome is a subjective decision made by the clinician ... based on the clinician's clinical experience,

the current diagnostic criteria and the effects of the unusual profile of abilities on the person's quality of life.

However, the value of the diagnosis should not be underestimated. It is not just a label but a passport or signpost for support and help, as well as a key to open the door to greater understanding and explanation.

In the UK, the government body, the National Institute for Health and Care Excellence (NICE), published its report entitled, 'Autism: recognition, referral, diagnosis and management of adults on the autism spectrum', No 142 (2012), suggesting, amongst many things, the National Health Service set up specialist multidisciplinary teams to carry out these diagnostic assessments and provide some care and support. The report also recommends five different assessment tools which all take a different tack in trying to identify the key features:

The DSM-5 identifies a number of criteria and areas of symptoms as prerequisites for a diagnosis.

- These symptoms must be present in the developmental period (early years).
- They must cause significant impairment in social or occupational functioning.
- They cannot be explained by other causes such as intellectual disability.

The range of symptoms is broken down into two main groups or domains.

Domain 1: Persistent deficit in social communication and social interaction across multiple contexts, which include the following:

(a) Deficits in social-emotional reciprocity, ranging, for example, from abnormal social approach and failure of normal back-and-forth conversation to reduced sharing of interests or emotions and failure to initiate or respond to social interactions.

(b) Deficits in non-verbal communication behaviours used for social interaction, including: poorly integrated verbal and non-verbal communication, abnormalities in eye contact and body language, deficits in understanding, use of gestures, lack of facial expressions and non-verbal communication.

(c) Deficits in developing, maintaining and understanding relationships, ranging, for example, from difficulties adjusting behaviour to suit various social contexts to difficulties sharing imaginative play or in making friends, and to absence of interest in peers.

Domain 2: Restricted, repetitive patterns of behaviour or interest or activities as manifested by at least two of the following.

(a) Stereotypical or repetitive motor movements, use of objects or speech (eg simple motor stereotypies, lining up toys or flipping objects, echolalia or idiosyncratic phrases)

(b) Insistence on sameness, inflexible adherence to routines or ritualised patterns or verbal or non-verbal behaviour (eg extreme distress at small changes, difficulty with transitions, rigid thinking patterns, greeting rituals, needing to take the same route or eat the same food everyday)

(c) Highly restricted, fixated interests that are abnormal in intensity or focus (eg strong attachment or preoccupation with unusual objects, excessively circumscribed or perseverative interests)

(d) Hyper- or hyporeactivity to sensory input or unusual interests in sensory aspects or the environment (eg apparent indifference to pain or temperature, adverse response to specific sounds or textures, excessive smelling or touching of objects, visual fascination with lights or movement).

2 The clinical interview – looking at the clients' personal history

The clinician assesses the clients' skills as they converse, but the assessment is usually broken down into two parts: first, the clinical interview looking in detail at the client's personal history and, second, examination of specific symptoms.

The clinical interview involves a number of areas of exploration which can be further broken down into a number of sections.

(a) Identifying the reasons for the referral for assessment: Identifying the reasons why the client at this point in their life has sought a diagnosis. What has happened? Was it the client's decision or has somebody else suggested it?

(b) Family history: This is an in depth look at the client's personal and family history. A typical question might be, 'Just paint a thumbnail sketch of the different members of your family saying something about the job they do, their personality and your relationship with them.' This is an open-ended question but is revealing on a number of counts. First, how the person answers the question. Are they succinct and able to get to the point, or do they miss the point or tend to ramble, providing unnecessary details? How does the client describe somebody else's personality? Many people with AS struggle with the concept, some people even saying, 'I don't know what you mean personality, he's just my dad'. Not being able to describe another personality might be an indicator of poor ToM.

(c) Current functioning and everyday activities: How does the client spend their time now? How independent are they in terms of everyday functioning and managing their lives? What are their future goals and aspirations?

(d) Neurodevelopmental history. Looking at information from the first few years of life:

- (i) Did the person as a child meet normal milestones such as walking and talking at the appropriate age, or was there a delay and idiosyncratic language use?
- (ii) Gaze and awareness of social world: did the client as a baby turn gaze when called by name, look to where the person pointed, look at people when they started talking, show an interest in other babies or children, or wave goodbye?
- (iii) Did they have sensory issues around being touched or sensitivity to noise? Did they like to be picked up, cuddled and enjoy physical affection?
- (iv) Did they have poor motor coordination or clumsiness?
- (v) Did they enjoy social reciprocal games such as 'peek-a-boo', that involve taking turns, or engage in imaginative or pretend play?
- (vi) Were they 'very laid back', easy-going babies who, for example, when waking up in their crib after a nap, did not cry out, but were content to entertain themselves?
- (vii) Was there an early liking of repetitive routines and inflexibility, or were they very 'picky eaters', and did they like to wear particular clothes or have unusual strong interests or attachments to unusual objects?
- (viii) Was there poor social awareness? For example, were they isolated, alone in the playground, without true friends, not meeting classmates outside school?
- (ix) Did they struggle to fit in with nursery school routines but had their own routine?
- (x) Did they have good attention to detail and a good memory?
- (xi) Did they have conversations just to be sociable (chit chat or small talk), or was their conversation restricted to getting their needs met or talking about special interests.

Sometimes the neurodevelopmental history points very directly towards a diagnosis, as in the case mentioned later. A mother accompanied her 36-year-old daughter to the assessment, describing her daughter's childhood in the following way.

> She was a quiet baby. If you picked her up, she would cry. She was happier if you laid her down and wrapped her up tightly in her blanket. She was a little late in walking, but once she did she just stood up and started walking. There wasn't much in between such as crawling. The same with talking and potty training; once she got the idea, she was absolutely perfect. Her first words weren't mummy or daddy as you would expect but, "Thomas the blue engine." When she started speaking she had a very strange tone and was very formal for a small child, a bit like an adult talking. She has grown out of that now. She was a happy child but very much in her own little world. If I left her she would just be happy to sit on a blanket playing with her toy cars or train. She didn't obviously see the consequences of something and if she was hot she didn't immediately see the sense in taking her cardigan off or if she was hungry didn't obviously see the sense of putting food in her mouth. She would get really upset – beside herself – with the sound of the hoover, or when her younger brother came along and he started crying. I was a little scared of her, because if something upset her, the reaction was always extreme – so for a lot of the time I felt that I was walking on eggshells. Things had to be a particular way or it would create a problem. She had to have all her buttons done up and her shoelaces fastened very, very tightly; otherwise there would be a tantrum. When she went to a party once she hadn't got the idea that you are supposed to smile and talk to people and she just sat in a chair in the corner on her own. At school she just focused on her work. I remember she was made "date monitor" at Primary School and the teacher said, 'She is the most reliable date monitor I've ever had in 20 years of being a teacher.' She actually got on much better with the adults and teachers than the children.

However, other parental testimonies are less obvious. Another parent said: 'I didn't notice anything; it all seemed quite normal. He was quiet, polite and happy to be on his own. He had a few unusual habits, but was the perfect child.' This could be for a variety of reasons: the child might have been very self-contained and compliant and slipped under the radar of detection; perhaps, there were other more boisterous siblings or peers distracting attention away; perhaps, the child escaped into its own internal world; perhaps, the parents themselves might have had some traits and didn't notice their offsprings' difficulties.

(e) Personal history: The next section involves the client telling their life story, broken down into childhood, school and education, employment, relationship history and any mental health issues, including other diagnoses.

For most people on the autistic spectrum life before getting a diagnosis is a struggle; people often comment, 'I always knew I was different but I didn't know why'. Many have a bewildering childhood and don't understand the logical social norms, fashions, and unwritten rules of social behaviour. 'When I went to nursery school it was odd because I didn't know what I was supposed to do. I just didn't get being a kid. I never understood the rules.' Isolation is a real problem illustrated by the comment, 'I'd be the one standing on his own in the playground'. Many AS people are teased and bullied at school which results in developing a low self-esteem. 'I was terrified for most of the time at school; I didn't know what was going to happen next. 'When I was a child I spoke like a little adult – I was never a child really. Children would come up to me and ask questions and I'd answer and they'd laugh.' One lady commented, 'When I was a child my family called me "Charlotte why", because I was always asking the question why – always wanting to understand things.' Because of poor coordination and impaired motor skills many struggle to be involved in team sports which add to the sense of exclusion. Many children are tricked and manipulated because of their naiveté about social relationships and a lack of ability to read other people's intentions.

One way to survive involves careful imitation and modelling, watching how other people manage. 'I worked out what other people wanted me to do, so I pretended to play.' One man recalled an event from his childhood which was particularly painful: 'I saw children running about in the playground hitting each other – they must have been playing tag – and I thought, that's how you make friends. So I started running around randomly hitting people and it was a disaster – I got told off by the teacher.' Some young AS children are very difficult but some are very easy. One mother commented: 'She was very easy, never any trouble, always happy to sit down and play with her toys. She was never interested in other children at tumble tots or nursery.'

3 Domain 1: Questions relating to social interaction and communication difficulties

The next two sections are an examination of some of the areas of questioning, discussion, observation of symptoms and clients' responses.

(a) Non-verbal: Is there a marked impairment in the use of multiple non-verbal behaviours such as eye-to-eye gaze, facial expression, body postures and gestures to regulate social interaction?

The assessor is looking for avoidance of eye contact or peculiar stiff gaze, use of gestures, clumsy gauche body language and limited or inappropriate facial expression. Appearances can be deceptive, and sometimes people will appear to have good eye contact but might be looking at a different part of the face. There is also a misconception that all AS people have poor eye contact which is not the case. Many adults with AS strive to conceal their non-verbal eccentricities and school themselves in overcoming gaze avoidance and may end up staring, or they may smile more than normal in an attempt to compensate for their lack of smiling or may deliberately use gestures and end up being very theatrical and overdemonstrative. Does the person use emphatic and descriptive gestures regularly to support spoken language (eg moving his hands in time with his speech), or is their body rather motionless?

- My eye contact has improved over the years but it's still uncomfortable, unnatural, too intrusive.
- I look at the tip of their nose, forehead or mouth.
- I don't know how long to look and end up staring.
- I pretend I'm reading the news on TV, looking up and then away.
- I used to get teased at school and called 'dead face', because my face doesn't have much expression.
- I'm told I've got a 'dead-pan' expression and don't use many gestures or facial expressions when I'm talking.
- I miss the point if someone communicates with non-verbals like raising an eyebrow.
- I've been told that I only use gestures when I'm angry and then I tend to point rather vigorously.

(b) Language and communication: Is there an unusual use or pattern of language and communication? Does the person use a pedantic style of speaking, either inclusion of too much, or too little detail?

There are a number of subtle, idiosyncratic, patterns of language and communication, which are often more obvious in children, but still have a vestige in adults. The individual may speak with a reduced or exaggerated intonation pattern or have difficulty modifying volume. Their ability to speak fluently may be impaired as they find it difficult to formulate language into a sentence. The choice of words may be overly formal or pedantic and the individual may not be able to modify their vocabulary to suit the social context; for example, they may speak to a child the same way as they would speak to an adult or speak to their boss in the same way as they would a member of their family. They may have a literal understanding of language, for example, when asked to 'take a seat'; they may think or sometimes say, 'Where shall I take it?'. Similarly, they may have difficulty understanding the implied meaning behind humour, sarcasm, innuendo and jokes. People with AS often like more obvious 'slapstick' humour or word puns rather than humour around social embarrassment or bizarre situations, where there is a need to understand the implied social meaning. Some adults may use neologisms (made-up words), for example, referring to dental floss as 'a flosser'.

Some people may not be able to understand what needs to be communicated, offering too much information or too little depending on the context. Many individuals report difficulty summarising ideas and this also tends to be reflected in their written medium. They may also relate events in an illogical order so that it is really difficult to work out the intended sequence. They may have difficulty staying on topic, with a tendency to go off on tangents. This is referred to as difficulty with 'topic maintenance'. Other difficulties include overuse of certain phrases, some of which are not entirely suited to the context. All these factors have a negative impact on the ability to have a two-way conversation.

- I find it difficult to judge how much or little people want to hear. People say to me, 'too much information'.
- I don't seem to be able to explain things succinctly. Instead I go all round the houses.
- I rarely give my opinions because they might not be quite right – not perfect. I have to sort things out in my head before I can say it.

(*continued*)

- At work people say my emails are a bit wordy. Instead of a one-liner, it becomes a one-pager.
- I know my voice is rather flat and monotonous.
- I find it difficult to modulate my voice; people often accuse me of shouting.
- When people say things incorrectly, it's annoying, but I try to bite my tongue. I am an extraordinarily good proofreader – it has to be exact.
- I take things very literally; you have to say exactly what you mean – no inferences.
- I don't like vague speech, such as the usual 'how are you', or 'maybe' or 'perhaps'.
- Either I haven't said a word or I've said a thousand too many. I can't gauge what people want.
- I carry a little book with me explaining idioms (eg 'pull your socks up').
- I don't get jokes, innuendo or sarcasm. I need people to talk directly and clearly and to say what they mean.
- My parents say I sounded like a little grown up when I was a child.
- I am really bad at explaining what I want done at work and get frustrated with junior staff because they don't do what I want.

(c) Friendships: Has the client failed to develop peer relationships appropriate to developmental level?

It is useful to explore what the word friendship means to the person and whether they understand the concept of building long-term relationships, having emotional attachments and reciprocal mutual support. Does the person have friends? How important are these friends? A further telltale sign is if the person's friends are either much older or younger, which might indicate that the person has difficulty compromising with same-age peers. People with AS often have a history of either (1) wanting to have friends but not knowing how to go about it or (2) a long-standing lack of interest in making friends.

- I find friendships difficult and tend not to bother with them.
- I don't relate to people my age; I get on better with children, older people or lame ducks.
- I prefer to do things on my own than with others.
- I do not enjoy social occasions.
- I hate 'outings', particularly to new places. I like my home – it's orderly.
- I might be friendly but I probably won't be your friend.
- I can't see the point of going out for coffee and 'catching up' ... what does it mean?
- I had a friend come around to the house once and I didn't know what to do. He ended up playing with my brother.
- I spend all my time in my room on my computer and don't have any real friends.

(d) Sharing/connecting: Is the client interested in communicating his/her experience to others? Do they spontaneously seek to share enjoyment, interests or achievements with other people?

This question is about the simple human desire to 'bring, show and tell'. For example, does the person want to share the experiences of their day over dinner or point out things of interest such as an interesting newspaper article, wanting to show and share? Does the person have a natural aloofness, only giving out information on a 'need-to-know basis', only needing people for a request, or talking about their special interest and having little interest in the other person?

- I live in my own little world.
- I communicate with my parents when we need to exchange information or if there is a problem.
- My mother says, getting anything out of me is like 'pulling teeth.'
- I've never celebrated any achievement; I just think 'so what?'.
- I don't need people, unless it's for a request.
- I've had three main relationships with women in my life and they all say to me, 'you're a closed book; you don't give yourself'. I've got no idea what they are talking about
- My worst nightmare was getting an award at work for my database and having to go to a swanky dinner – I didn't want to talk to them.

(e) Reciprocal social interaction: Is there a lack of social and emotional reciprocity (eg not knowing how to comfort someone; lack of empathy). Are there difficulties in understanding social situations and other people's thoughts and feelings?

The term 'reciprocity' comes from the Latin *reciprocus*, meaning, 'returning the same way' or 'alternating'. This question is tapping the two-way process of social and emotional relationships, the to-and-fro, backwards and forwards interaction between two people. People with AS often do not have such conversations and report that they don't know what to say, how to start a conversation, when to talk, when to respond or how to shift a conversation from one topic to another. The person with AS might talk at (instead of with) others. Part of having a conversation is the ability to interpret social cues, to pick up on the emotions of the other person and to respond appropriately. Does the person have the ability to understand the rules, nuances and contexts of social situations, to pick up intentions and emotions in other people, interpret the expression on the other's face, posture, tone and read between the lines? If they recognise the other person is upset, do they have the ability to respond appropriately? If they identify that the person is bored, can they act sensitively and change the topic of conversation? Do they struggle to keep up in social situations, avoiding parties, where there is a lack of structure and prefer formal structured situations? Are social situations an effort, leaving individuals with AS tired and in need of a period of isolation to recharge the batteries? Do they manage limited social situations by time-limiting them, or do they manage being much more comfortable on a one-to-one basis but struggle in groups? Do they struggle with rapid interchange, shifting subject matter, banter and other people's humour, sarcasm and jokes?

- I find it hard to keep a two-way conversation going.
- I can't work out when it's my turn to talk and I can never think of what to say.
- I find it difficult to work out people's intentions and read between the lines.
- I can't keep track of conversations in a group situation – it moves too fast. I'll often say, 'just go back to what you were saying about ...'
- I'm told that I talk at people; it's not really a two-way conversation – I have to say what I think.
- I can't read people's subtle emotions. I understand crying or shouting, but it's the emotions in between I struggle with.
- I feel very uncomfortable around people who are upset. I am quite good in a crisis because I stay calm and think rationally, but I'm not very good at putting an arm around anybody.

(*continued*)

- When my sister was upset I didn't know what to do. I just sat in silence and stared at the floor. I didn't know what to say. I thought, I shall put my arm around her and then thought how long this is going to go on for?
- I avoid all social events at work; otherwise I get labelled as a weirdo.

(f) Consideration and awareness of others: Is there a tendency to turn any conversation back on to self or own topic of interest? Is there an inability to recognise when the listener is interested or bored? Is there a frequent tendency to say things without considering the emotional impact on the listener (faux pas)?

Not appreciating or being interested in the other person's point of view or interests stems from having difficulty holding two things in mind at the same time – self and other. Does the person tend to monopolise conversations, talking at length about their special interests or opinions and not engage in turn-taking when speaking? The skill of recognising if the other person is interested or bored involves being able to identify the verbal and non-verbal behaviour of another person. Often the person with AS will not use 'check out' statement such as, 'Am I making sense?', 'Do you follow me?' or 'Do you know what I mean?'. Sometimes the person with AS doesn't recognise that the other person is not interested, or they might notice but simply just carry on talking regardless.

Does the person have a tendency to make inappropriate comments, make faux pas, drop a clanger, making comments that might hurt or upset the other person? This is often about being too blunt and honest, revealing inner thoughts and feelings without putting it through a 'mental censor' or 'socially acceptable filter'. Again the difficulty could be due to not being able to hold two things in mind at the same time – you and the other person. The social world is made up of a complex network of unspoken rules that need to be negotiated. The person may feel that it is essential to be honest and not believe in or understand the need for social niceties and the occasional 'little white lie'.

- People often tell me that I go on and on about the same thing.
- I'm too blunt and say things that upset people but there is no malice aforethought ... I don't mean to.
- If somebody is talking I am raring to go, desperate to find a gap and talk about what I want to talk about.
- I tend to focus on my own thoughts rather than on what the listener might be thinking.
- I'm not very good at picking up subtle cues. I'm OK with the obvious, like if they walk out or fall asleep, I know that they're bored.
- I don't really care if they are not interested. I've got to say it and carry on talking.
- People say I talk at them, not to them.
- My friend said, 'you go too far'. But I never know how far too far is.
- I would not be a good diplomat – wars would start.
- I often offend people. Truth is one thing that people often don't like.
- I am 100 per cent open and honest and can't lie, not even a 'little white lie', which upsets people.
- I don't really get political correctness. I'm always putting my foot in it. It just comes out of my mouth before the social filter kicks in.
- I can't tell if I've upset Nicky until I see tears on her face.
- I once said to a man, 'why do you have such a big fat belly'.

(g) Small talk: Is there impairment in the ability to initiate or sustain a conversation with others? The person cannot see the point of superficial social contact, niceties or passing time with others, unless there is a clear discussion point/debate or activity.

Adults with AS often say that they are poor at 'small talk' or 'chit-chat' or they might say they have learned to do it, but don't see the point in it. Small talk and chit-chat are usually engaged in to establish rapport, or to acknowledge the presence of another person, or for the simple pleasure of communicating and interacting with another human being. There is no specific purpose, no defined goal; it is often spontaneous, not planned and often the person with AS is not very good at it.

- I can't see the point of small talk; it seems like a complete waste of time. I'd rather be discussing something important.
- Going to the hairdresser and having to talk to him is more stressful than having three men with guns trying to kill me.
- I frequently find that I don't know how to keep a conversation going
- I only speak when I need to speak.
- Why would you talk about the weather when you already know what it's like?
- I get bored with conversations that don't contain information.
- I'd rather cut off my ears than make small talk.
- I don't chat. On Monday morning I say, 'Where is the work?'
- I've learned a little script over the years and will say, 'How are you?' and make a comment about the weather.

4 Domain 2: Questions relating to restricted, repetitive patterns of behaviour

(a) Special interests: Does the person have encompassing preoccupation with one or more stereotyped and restricted patterns of interest that is abnormal either in intensity or focus? Do they have all absorbing narrow special interests?

Does the person have special interests that are all encompassing, time consuming, that are rather narrow in range, intense, rigid and often involve repetition learning and categorising? These are subjects that the person knows a great deal about, are rather like obsessions, where the person becomes totally immersed in the subject to the exclusion of all else. As a child there may have been an interest in collecting, categorising or learning systems of information such as all the capital cities, fossils, Star Trek, Dr Who, Lego or Thomas the Tank Engine. We need to bear in mind the difference between really liking something and being obsessed with it. Liking *Lord of the Rings* is normal, but if a 30-year-old has watched all the films 25 times each and knows the plot in the minutest detail, it might be considered extreme – an all-encompassing preoccupation. The special interest is a great form of relaxation, taking the person away from the stresses of the social and emotional world.

- To me my special interest is like a proper love affair. I love it. One of the reasons I married my husband was because he was also interested in Egyptology.
- If I didn't have responsibilities all I'd do all day is play on the computer and play with Lego. For a 36-year-old man, I like Lego too much. My wife bribes me to go shopping with her saying she'll buy me Lego.

(*continued*)

- I frequently get so strongly absorbed in one thing that I lose sight of other things.
- If I get an interest I have to collect information and research it to bits and completely understand it.
- I've always loved maps and road systems. For my sixteenth birthday treat my parents drove me around the M 25.
- I get hooked into things and become totally obsessed and have to know everything; then I move on and it's something else.
- I am totally obsessed with the North American fur trade between 1860 and 1880.
- I liked Thomas the Tank Engine because each train had got its own colour, number and name; they all had set personalities that don't alter and are quite predictable.

(b) Routines and rituals: Is there an inflexible adherence to specific, non-functional routines or rituals? Does the person get upset when the way they like to do things is suddenly changed?

People with AS usually like routine, structure, predictability, sameness and get locked into schedules, and have a strong need to do things over and over again. This might be noticeable in areas such as choice of food, clothes and routines. They like to know where they are going and what is ahead and don't like change, unpredictability and randomness. Once settled into a routine there is an aspect of soothing and calming. Any interruption or disruption to that routine is stressful. These routines and rituals may involve eating patterns, washing, how their environment is organised, clothes, taking the same route to work or performing an activity in a strict sequence. Routines are a structure and methodical system providing a set of rules, a timetable, a task to do, a list, a goal, a set of bullet points, precision, measurement. These rules and routines are carried out because they bring pleasure and soothing, in a world that can be chaotic and overstimulating.

- My life is ruled by lists, sub-lists, goals and bullet points.
- I prefer to do things over and over in the same way.
- I need structure and plans and if somebody interrupts it the whole day is ruined.
- I don't like food touching on a plate. I keep it separate and eat it separately. A wet vegetable like broccoli, next to chips, would ruin the texture, making the chips soggy.
- If I go into town I need to know in what order we are going to go into shops and how long we are going to be there and when we are going into McDonalds. If the order goes wrong I throw a massive tantrum.
- I need to know what is coming next. Holidays have to be well planned – my route in the supermarket is planned. I don't like change to my routine.
- I love playing the scales on my piano and like Mozart and Baroque music because it's neat, has steady beat, phasing, regular intervals so you know where you are. I don't like people like Wagner or Beethoven who are more dramatic and all over the place.
- When I'm cooking I measure things out on the scales very precisely, chop things very finely in the right way and always use a stop watch to time cooking.
- I always wear the same black clothes and always wear tracksuit bottoms for comfort.

(c) Repetitive movement: Stereotyped and repetitive motor mannerisms (eg rocking, hand or finger flapping or twisting)

There is an image of people with classic autism, with a learning disability in an institution, with a tendency to self-sooth by rocking backwards and forwards or banging their heads repetitively. Traces or milder forms of these behaviours can often be seen in adults with AS. These behaviours are called 'self-stims', which the person engages in to either rev themselves up if they are understimulated, or to calm themselves down when they are overstimulated. The rocking, spinning, flapping, finger fiddling and knee shaking are physical bodily manifestations of a routine or ritual as there is an element of repetition, sameness and soothing.

- I like rocking; I always rock myself to sleep.
- As a child I used to spend a lot of time spinning. Now I just do a slight rocking. It's comfortable and nice. I don't know I'm doing it until somebody points it out.
- I make noises to myself like 'uurm ...', 'urm ...', like the noise of the car.
- If I get excited or stressed I flap my hands.
- I have this thing where I twist my hair all the time.
- I bite my nails and flap my hands when I get stressed.
- My leg shakes and I crack my knuckles when I feel anxious.
- I wear a soft chewable necklace, called chewllery, which I chew instead of chewing my hands or fingers.

(d) Attention to detail: Is there a persistent preoccupation with parts of objects or system – to focus on the details rather than the overall idea or picture?

This is the ability to have an exceptional 'eye for detail', to notice and remember numbers, facts and information that other people don't. The memory part of the brain is particularly efficient, absorbing detail and literally having an 'eagle eye'. The person might become totally immersed in the details of something, hyperfocusing to the exclusion of all else, being unable to switch or divide attention or see the bigger picture. Having an eye for detail links to the underlying desire to understand systems or the rules that govern a topic.

- I usually notice car number plates and other strings of information.
- I can remember every phone number, password or door code I've known.
- I'm not very good at multitasking, or standing back – because I get sucked into details.
- I will shop for an item by remembering the barcode.
- At work they called me 'the error police' or 'the red line police' as I would notice errors on duty charts, or spelling mistakes would leap off the page. I always excelled at writing down policies and procedure documents and believe in being pedantic.
- I used to like to line up the second hands of all the clocks in the house so they were exactly the same, but my overall awareness of time is appalling.
- I could look at a document and scan it with my eyes, all the typos, spelling and punctuation mistakes jump out and I wouldn't be able to let them go.
- If I get interested in something I have to learn everything about it like Taekwando.
- I know the bus timetables for the whole of Plymouth.
- My tutor said, 'I'm not interested in that blade of grass; I want you to paint me a garden.'

(e) Rigid thinking: Is there a tendency to think of issues as being black and white (eg in politics or morality), rather than considering multiple perspectives in a flexible way?

This is the tendency to have strong, single-minded opinions about things, to think in a binary or digital way. They are black or white, right or wrong, yes or no, 0 or 1. This thinking pattern is rigid and inflexible. There is little middle ground, shades of grey or flexibility. This often means that the person needs to do a job properly, needs to always complete or finish something; there are no half measures or cutting corners; everything is all or nothing. This lack of flexibility means that the person with AS is often not very good at taking in and absorbing a different view, or changing their feelings about something. The rules become set like concrete and the person becomes a prisoner to them. This can lead to a strong sense of justice, falling out with people, emotional explosions when the rules aren't kept or somebody else has conflicting views.

- When people say, 'We'll have to agree to disagree', it drives me absolutely mad.
- With me it's either one or the other. I'm either mad or OK.
- Everything to me is polar. I am the most polar man in the universe. In my head everything is right or wrong. I never say 'Oh I'm not sure'.
- Once I've learned a rule I won't break it. I'd never walk on the grass if there was a sign saying not to.
- I've been called a bit of a Hitler, because I think that if you drop some litter you should be punished.
- I hate autumn when the leaves are half off the trees – I'd rather they were all off or all on as in winter or summer.
- I like rules. You know where you stand with rules.
- My wife was pregnant and needed to get to the hospital quickly, but I couldn't go above the speed limit.

(f) Sensory issues: Does the person have sensory sensitivities and motor coordination problems? (see chapter 7)

Sensory sensitivities or 'sensory integration disorder' are becoming increasingly recognised as significant problems for people with AS.

Maybe there is an oversensitivity or undersensitivity with the seven main senses: touch, taste, smell, sight, hearing, coordination and balance. For example, it is common for people with sensitivity to touch, to remove the labels from clothes or avoiding wearing a particular type of material, like wool. The person with AS might not like the texture of particular foodstuffs and be 'fussy eaters'. They might have a strong adverse reaction to loud noises such as fireworks, a hoover or fire sirens. There might be problems with movement and balance, or a problem with the positional sense of where the body is in time and space known as 'proprioception'. Other unusual sensory issues might be a very low pain threshold or not being aware of body temperature, which means the person might wear a T-shirt in winter. It is very common for people with sensory problems to feel 'overloaded' very quickly and need to remove themselves from the overstimulating environment. However, some sensory sensitivities can result in the person developing a particular skill, such as having perfect pitch and an exceptional musical ability.

- I often notice small sounds when others do not.
- I always cut the labels out of my clothes.
- I can't stand the sound of a bell or alarm or the noise people make when they eat.
- I don't like being touched softly – it burns, it hurts. I'd rather be squeezed firmly.
- When I feel overwhelmed by my senses, I have to isolate myself to shut them down.
- I wear clothes for comfort, not fashion. Wool is the devil and I hate velvet!
- I wear sunglasses and earplugs.
- Sometimes touch is a problem because it's a massive distraction and if I'm at full mental capacity I haven't got time to cope with it.

(*continued*)

> - I could never tell whether I'm full or hungry and I never feel too hot or cold.
> - I can easily recall the pitch of a tuning fork five minutes after its sounded – I have perfect pitch.
> - I shake people's hand with gritted teeth.
> - If someone is talking and there is background noise I have to turn it off.
> - I'm always knocking things over, can't catch a ball to save my life and was always falling off my bike when I was a child.
> - I could never dance or do aerobics or even swimming. I just couldn't coordinate left and right. Someone said I had bilateral coordination problems.

(g) Imagination: Does the person have the imagination necessary for engaging in imaginative or spontaneous creative thinking or play, or to be able to make up or generate a spontaneous story? Is there a lack of interest in fiction (written, or drama)?

Children with AS often are not very good at playing equally and reciprocally with another in an imaginative, pretend or make-believe way. For example, they might not be able to ascribe a character to a plastic doll, or to imagine a broom stick as a rifle or a spear. Imagination is the faculty or action of forming new ideas, images or concepts of external objects not present to the senses. One man said, insightfully, 'I can't imagine anything – it has to be right in front of me'. Instead of imaginary play children with AS like routines and repetitive play such as lining up cars or books, playing with constructional toys such as Lego or playing board games with set rules. Similarly, adults might not be very good at telling a bedtime story to a child by plucking something straight out of imagination. One task often used in the assessment is to ask the person to make up a story out of a handful of random objects.

The usual pattern for somebody with AS is to avoid reading fiction or novels about emotion and relationships, preferring to read science fiction, fantasy or horror stories, which is a genre one step removed from real life. For example, 'Lord of the Rings' is a typical AS book with lots of intricate details, a formulaic plot, with little emotional depth or explanation of why people do things. Characters have traumatic experiences – go to hell or Mordor and back – but emotionally are just the same as when they started. There is also a tendency to read factual books, watch documentaries and a preference for visiting a museum rather than going to the theatre. Although, it is now recognised that females might tend to read fiction more than males to learn more about relationships and socialising. Often a favourite book or film is read or watched repeatedly.

- I couldn't play at having a tea party with a bear and a doll because in my mind that's just stupid.
- My sister would play with dolls but to me they were just plastic things.
- I love space and technic Lego but couldn't build anything spontaneous like my brother. I'd have to follow the instructions. I couldn't make something from nothing, but give me instructions and I can produce something beautifully crafted.
- The word imagination fills me with dread.
- At school, in a music leson, we once did jazz improvisation and the teacher asked me to improvise 'Take the A Train'. I just couldn't do it, yet I could play the clarinet fluently to Grade 8 standard. I was absolutely lost. It was so embarrassing I just broke down.
- In ballet the teacher said, 'Do a 30-second improvised movement'. I couldn't think what to do and just rocked from foot to foot and everybody laughed.
- I'd rather do a hundred sums than write a story. Making something up is very difficult for me.

(*continued*)

- I have never had any interest in things that were not real. Why would you read fiction when you could read something that was real and you could get something out of it?
- As I child I was always found with my nose in a book – usually about natural history or dinosaurs.
- I watch soap operas on TV and try to model my life on the characters.
- I have seen *Lord of the Rings* and the Harry Potter films over 50 times each.

Chapter Four

The journey from discovery to acceptance

1 Telling the story

It is important for people with a new diagnosis of AS to be able to tell their own stories. This may help them to make sense of their condition, create an internal narrative, impose a structure and gain an understanding of themselves. It is also important to hear other people's stories, their journeys, struggles, similar problems and ways of coping. For most people, a late diagnosis can be a turning point in their lives, a change in perception. There is a journey of self-discovery and acceptance. For most people it's good to know that they are not alone and that there are many other people on a similar pathway.

Up until 1987, there were only three published autobiographies of people with an ASD. Between 2003 and 2008, there were 30 more published and since then there have been many more. The narrative structure of most of these books is that the path is difficult but things do get better. Liane Holliday Willey's book *Pretending to Be Normal* (1999) suggests that autistic traits continue to fade away, whereas Temple Grandin's book *Thinking in Pictures* (1995) seems to say: 'Autism is part of who I am. I am a condition of hope not a disorder.' In this chapter are nine different stories about the journey of diagnosis written by adults with AS, in the first few years following their diagnoses.

2 Kate's story: 'Diagnosis stabilised my mental health'

Why am I different? Why can't I be like the others? Why am I always in trouble when I'm not being naughty? Why am I so useless? These were the questions that were a running commentary while I was young. I didn't understand how I could understand mathematical concepts so much earlier and quicker than others but couldn't figure out how to join in at playtimes. I was incredibly lucky that I was sent to a very small school and there wasn't any bullying. I would watch the groups playing or just stand on the edge, not joining in. I did have friends but I could only normally engage with one at a time and felt left out very quickly if there were more. I used to be sent on holidays with French families in the summers and everyone used to think I was homesick, but I wasn't missing my parents. It took me a long time to figure out what was upsetting and challenging me – which was the change in routine, not knowing what we were doing and when.

These feelings carried on as an adult. I became very depressed as I couldn't figure out why I found life so difficult. I was labelled as spoilt, attention seeking or even having borderline personality disorder. I was frequently told that as I was highly intelligent I didn't need to have angry outbursts, meltdowns or shutdowns. Often I'd have meltdowns because I couldn't make anyone understand what I was feeling. How could I? I didn't know what it all meant or what I was actually feeling myself.

In early adulthood my life gradually came undone. I could not get out of the depression and thought it was better to die than to live like that. It was after a serious suicide attempt that I saw a psychologist who specialised in diagnosing adults with Asperger's syndrome. The Community Mental Health Team, whom I had been seeing, had had enough of me and had nothing left to offer and just saw me as a nuisance – they didn't think I had Asperger's.

I remember being able to talk to the psychologist – I'd found a YouTube clip of him so I knew what he looked like! I even managed to ignore his rather chaotic room (organised chaos, he told me!). The experience was interesting and actually quite enjoyable and the ethos was that although I might think and behave differently from most people, that is all it was – different, not wrong. For the first time in a long time, I felt that I was valued. It was so important to me that I could ask questions as we went along. At the end he told me that I was definitely Asperger's. I felt I could breathe. With his explanation, how I felt all my life made sense. It gave me 'permission' to feel how I did, to find life as confusing as I did.

Afterwards when I told my parents, I remember them saying that they felt guilty as they believed I was just naughty and difficult. We had to draw a line – they couldn't have done anything different, because in those days people didn't know about Asperger's. They did what they thought was right at the time and let's face it, I am difficult, Asperger's or not!

The diagnosis has helped in so many ways. With a diagnosis, medical professionals seem to listen when I explain why something is so hard. It has made me more aware of triggers and I have accepted that I need to remove myself from situations that I know are difficult to handle. Most of the time I can tell myself that I am 'allowed' to feel like I am but other times I still revert to the thought, 'I'm intelligent, why can't I change this?'.

I can honestly say that my diagnosis was the best thing that has happened. Whilst I still get frustrated that I can't deal with certain things, I am able to be kinder to myself, most of the time. I do not shy away from telling anyone who is involved in my life that I have Asperger's. The choir that I sing in accepts me as I am. I do not expect people to fully understand, but if they can give me space and some support that's fine. What I would really like this world to know is that just because I am intelligent, it does not mean that I 'choose' to act the way I do when it is all too much and I am overwhelmed; too much noise, too much light; too much socialising! I have lived with my parents for the last few years and the diagnosis has certainly helped. My parents now realise that I am not necessarily unsociable but I need that down time when I come home from work. They also accept that I need routine and clear instructions. The anxiety, which we now realise, is more to do with the Asperger's than the depression is more successfully managed by understanding the need for structures and warnings about change.

I believe that I am now getting the support I need due to my official diagnosis and people are making adjustments. For those that believe diagnosing an adult serves no purpose, I totally disagree as I believed that it stabilised my mental health and saved my life.

3 Joanna's story: 'Drafting a map to chart my course'

When I was 10 years old, we were driving through Colorado on a family holiday when my dad spotted a snowy hillside that was just perfect for sledging. We didn't have any sledges with us, so my dad fashioned some by unclipping the lids of our suitcases. On my first run, I realised why suitcase lids were not sold as sledges – they have no steering – and I hit an enormous bank of snow. Tumbling headfirst, I entered the snowdrift and was buried six feet deep. Inside, all was white. I was stunned and had lost all points of reference; I couldn't tell which way was up. Even today it feels as though I was under that snow for hours, although it could not have been more than seconds as my father plunged in and pulled me out.

I often remember this event when thinking about my diagnosis of Asperger's syndrome. Feeling my father's hand grasping the back of my T-shirt and hauling me out into the sunshine is very like the day my psychologist told me I was on the autism spectrum. From that moment, I began to make sense of the difficulties I had always experienced, to piece together a way to live my life. For me, the neurotypical world is still as unnavigable as that Colorado snowdrift, but I am beginning to draft a map that will help me chart my course.

Routines have always been important to me. Whenever possible I do the same things in the same order for the same length of time. I wear the same clothes (making multiple purchases of items I like to wear), eat the same foods, do the same hobbies. I try not to worry that this behaviour is unusual by neurotypical standards; repetition is calming and helps me to keep equilibrium as other areas of my life, such as work, are not so easy to order. There are times when I can't follow my daily routine, but I have put into place strategies to manage the stress this inevitably causes.

More than disruptions to routine, interactions with people are an enormous source of stress for me. I rarely know what to say in any given situation and find that I take what is said at face value, unable to infer meanings, which often frustrates neurotypical speakers. I find it very challenging to be in conversation with more than one participant. The talk ping-pongs around; I am never sure who will speak next and when it will be my turn to say something. Even now I do not know how to join groups of people at a meeting or party and when I do find myself in a group, I don't pick up on the signal that they are going to disburse – discovering myself standing alone with everyone gone!

As a result of these trials, I limit my exposure to neurotypical events, one per week as a maximum where possible and keep my time spent in a social situation short – two hours is my absolute limit. I have a small group of people with whom I feel comfortable, people who understand my need for clear communication and are happy to spend time in silence as well. It helps that these people like to engage in the activities I enjoy and are happy for me to retreat if feeling overwhelmed. I also find friendship and support in online forums for people on the autism spectrum.

Food shopping is a sensory nightmare – overlit, overstocked supermarkets clogged with people, trollies and children conspire to overwhelm me so I have learned to go during quiet periods. I always take a list, organised according to the store layout. The self-scan and pack system is useful as I don't have to engage with a cashier. Buying clothes is another ordeal and one which I conquer by shopping online. I can search for the items I need, filtering according to colour, fabric and size. I can try the items on in the comfort of my own home and return those that are not suitable.

I am fortunate that I have found a job that suits my need for routine and is limited in the need to deal with people. Managing a database plays to my skills; it requires attention to detail, accuracy and focus. I am more than happy to undertake repetitive tasks and often perform data analysis, which I really enjoy. I work in a very small office that is quiet, calm and has muted lighting. Perfume is my biggest issue at work. I can tolerate light, fresh scents but musky perfumes are simply too strong. I counter this by using a coconut hand cream and rubbing a small amount under my nostrils. It is not perfect, but I do find that the smell of perfume lessens as the day goes on.

With all the challenges of living in a neurotypical world, it is important for me to have an array of strategies for stress and anxiety reduction. Every day I must take time to decompress. I need to retreat into the sanctuary that is my peaceful, uncluttered home with its neutral colour scheme and lack of strong smells or bright lights. I like to enjoy the sound of silence or quiet talk radio. I will read during this time or crochet, a wonderfully repetitive and rhythmic activity.

I often think I should take shares in a camomile tea producer as I drink such a lot of it! The camomile has a calming effect but, more than that, the ritual of making tea, as the Chinese have known for centuries, is relaxing in itself. Even holding a warm cup – I have a smooth-surfaced pottery mug with a handle that is just the right size – is restorative.

I practise Qigong, a form of Tai Chi, for 20 minutes every morning. Slow movements, coupled with the focus on deep, 'belly' breathing, relax the body during practise but the effects of the Qigong continue throughout the day as I find myself pausing to breathe or focus on a physical task.

This mindfulness calms my thoughts and brings me into the present moment; I am so often living in the past or worrying about the future. Ten minutes meditation follows my Qigong practise. I try to clear my mind and remember that thoughts are simply that – just thoughts.

Walking is another activity that alleviates stress for me. I am sure my neighbours think I am mad as I follow the same 30-minute route each day, rain or shine.

I find that I am sensitive to sugar and additives in food. My stress and anxiety are much worse if the things I eat are processed, so I enjoy a 'clean' diet. I eat little and often to maintain an optimum blood sugar level.

I ensure that I always carry a kit with a set of headphones, hand-sanitiser (the thought of germs causes me a great deal of stress), coconut hand cream to mask strong smells, snacks and water. With my kit, I can manage most sensory issues and if I can't, I give myself permission to leave.

With careful organisation and planning I am increasingly able to keep my stress and anxiety under control. I operate under the motto KISS: Keep it simple, stupid! While I'd love to be a captain of industry or high-flying politician, I now accept that I have limits. After all, a successful life is a life well lived and by taking care of the Asperger's needs I have, I am finding that I am getting more pleasure from doing less with less stress.

4 David's story: 'Everything is different but nothing has changed'

I always felt different and remember thinking I'd been dropped by a spaceship and one day they would come and collect me. For a number of years as a child, I got really interested in astronomy and put my bed by the window so I could look up at the stars. I didn't fit in at school; I was always the last to be picked in team games and at play time you'd find me standing on my own by the fence or I just sat and read a book in the library. I was bullied by both pupils and staff but I was good at maths and sciences. In an English lesson, one homework assignment was to write an essay on 'The humour of Jane Austin'. My essay was very short but very honest and I wrote, 'There is no humour, she's not funny'. The teacher's response was to get angry, give me a detention, send me to the headmaster and afterwards mimic me – I thought she was unfair as I was only giving my honest answer.

I've seen counsellors and therapists over the years who mainly diagnosed me as having a social phobia and depression. They explained that social phobia was being scared of what people were thinking of you and worried that you would make a mistake. That wasn't my experience, but I couldn't explain what it was that made me unable to communicate with strangers. I also had some sensory issues such as being overwhelmed by loud noise, bright lights and uncomfortable clothes.

Despite everything I eventually got married to a very caring lady called Claire who worked as a nurse. I had a job in IT as a customer service engineer for a large company. I was surprisingly successful and won regional and national prizes, although I always avoided Christmas parties, trips to the pub or firms' days out. To me the work was problem solving – all very logical and binary. People would ring in with an IT problem and it was simply a question of analysis and diagnosis. I would ask questions and they would answer yes or no – no middle ground, no shades of grey, no complicated emotions.
I was so successful I was promoted to team lead and given managerial responsibilities – that's where it all started to go wrong. I couldn't cope with understanding other people's issues and conflicts and I

got depressed and ended up in a psychiatric hospital – which was a nightmare. Claire had read an article on Asperger's and discussed it with the psychiatrist who made a referral.

Eventually, after a long wait, I saw a psychologist who carried out a detailed autism/Asperger's assessment. He went through my whole life history, seemed to understand and had a questionnaire completed by my mother. Claire was present and I remember her holding my hand a couple of times. It was a relief when he said that I'd got Asperger's syndrome, but no great surprise. However, I was surprised at how emotional I was: Claire hugged me and I felt a tear on my cheek as I shook hands with the psychologist – I felt that I'd got an answer at last.

From that moment onwards everything was different although nothing obviously changed. I felt as if somebody had turned the lights on. I thought and dreamed vividly about my past and all the incidents that could now be explained by my condition. It was like I was re-experiencing my life through the prism of autism. I told a few people and generally got a good reaction although I felt my sister and her husband scrutinising me – leaving me feeling a little self-conscious. The best reaction was from my manager at work who surprisingly said, 'I feel honoured that you've told me'. With the help of HR we managed to restructure my job so I was without any managerial responsibilities – earning less money, but I didn't care – it felt like a great improvement.

I think getting the diagnosis six years ago has stabilised my life. I saw the psychologist who helped me unravel what was the Asperger's and what was depression. It helped me unravel who and why I am. I still see that psychologist about once every nine months which helps as I know there is someone out there who would understand me if the stresses build up. As I read in a book once, I see the diagnosis as a signpost not a label. It indicated where I've come from and gives me some direction of where I'm going. Claire has helped enormously – she is my social eyes and ears – I would struggle without her. I must be difficult to live with as I don't really like going out much and don't like holidays. Claire said, 'Why don't we go to the Grand Canyon for your birthday?'. My reaction was: 'It's just a big ditch, what's the point, why don't we watch the video.' I'd rather stay at home for a week, go running, play my guitar, work on the house and garden and on my birthday watch a film and have a takeaway pizza. The diagnosis has helped me accept who I am and helped me to stop 'trying to be normal' and doing things that I don't want to do. Everything has changed but nothing is different.

5 Rachel's story: 'Diagnosis has been a gift'

I was always a quiet and solitary child, although I didn't want to be, and at times the loneliness was overwhelming. I had a very abusive home life and escaped into books and solitude and created my own imaginary world. I used to stimm regularly and was noted as being odd, but it was blamed on my mother's mental illness. Friends were few and far between, but after about age eight I was able to maintain a solid friendship with another child whose father had terminal cancer. She was used to the unusual and was able to be friends with me. When I was 18, I made another friend who taught me the basics of social skills, such as the value of asking questions and listening for answers.

My daughter was diagnosed as autistic at age four, but it had been apparent since she was two, but because she was so similar to me I did not understand the concerns. Once she was diagnosed I realised that autism is written about differently to the way I experience it. I 'do what I do'. I am me. So to see my behaviour and personality presented as wrong, abnormal and dysfunctional was very isolating. For example, as an adult I am quite gregarious and like being with people up to a point, but socialising is exhausting and I can only manage a certain amount, and then I need my space. I do occasionally make the odd social slip up, but by and large I can usually unpick social situations. I count seconds of eye contact, closely mimic others and have to plan conversations. It always surprises me that other people are so bothered about clothes and make-up. I don't think I'm stuck in rigid routines: this does not fit my experience.

Before the assessment I had to fill in questionnaires and give one to my mother which proved to be quite difficult. She kept on saying, 'Oh it doesn't look good does it Rachel?'. Her experience was so different to mine as I saw getting a diagnosis as a positive thing. I'd hoped it might relieve some of her guilt as I was such an odd child (flapping hands, singing myself to sleep whilst rocking my head, didn't walk until I was two and no friends). I'd hoped for understanding and possibly some healing with Mum, but that was not to be.

The assessment was really thorough and took about three hours. I remember a very sweaty seat and counting the bricks repetitively on a building opposite the clinician's office. They made a particularly interesting pattern around some windows in groups of seven – my favourite number to count to. I was really surprised to get a full diagnosis of autistic spectrum disorder (Asperger's syndrome) as I expected to be diagnosed with just having traits. When it was over, I phoned my other half and said, 'Guess what, I'm autistic!'. He answered 'so what's new' and that was that, no drama, just carrying on. I was quite disorientated after three hours and had to work out the way to walk. I felt quite vulnerable and frightened as I suddenly twigged that I simply can't hide that I struggle so much socially any more. I bumped into a man I knew who had two autistic twins and told him, and he said something jocular like, 'so you're a nutter now too'. I enjoyed the light-heartedness of it as it stopped me from brooding. I managed to navigate myself home on the bus and hugged my children. I also wrote a message on Facebook informing all my friends that I'd got the diagnosis, but that I wasn't about to start hiding and although I knew I was as mad as a box of frogs, I was still part of this world and intended to stay so. Gratifyingly everyone that posted was hugely supportive and several just posted 'croak', which made me smile lots. I felt so honoured that people were prepared to stay with me. I've also realised that socialising on Facebook suits me much better than face-to-face contact as it's much less exhausting and it gives you much more time to work out the social rules.

Now, two years later, I think that an autism diagnosis is the gift that keeps on giving! I am not sure how I would have felt if I had been given it as a child as the emphasis seems to be on the negatives. It would have been lovely for someone to say to me: 'It's OK not to be social, you can trust yourself and follow your special interest.' But, when I was younger, I felt I needed to be a more well-rounded person, based on the many personal criticisms and bullying I received. I have learned mindfulness and feel more in charge of the way I respond to my thoughts. I also still take a low-dose SSRI which helps with the anxiety arising from my sensory processing disorder. This helps me be a better parent as I really struggle with the noise that the children make.

Knowing I am autistic has freed me to be myself. I can rejoice in being quirky and different as I actually am. It is great knowing that it is the shape of my brain that determines this as opposed to me being a dunce and wilfully not understanding stuff. It's great to embrace the huge feeling of joy and love my special interest engulfs me in, and enjoy it just for that, instead of berating myself for not pushing it further. It is great to understand more about sensory issues and use them to my advantage – long walks in the woods, weighted blankets and just the right music for my mood. It's wonderful to finally understand what sort of person I am.

The gifts it's given me as a parent are immense. I will share my children's special interests, I WON'T stop them stimming; I love them for being their quirky selves and best of all I can choose to present their unique neurology as a positive. I never understood why society makes such a fuss about difference – I suffer from face blindness and struggle to recognise people. Most people seem to run with the crowd for their protection which makes them practically invisible to me. Difference means I can see them and this should be celebrated. Difference is not a threat to the crowd but an added dimension to humanity.

6 Floyd's story: 'My role models are James Bond and Bertie Wooster'

Throughout my life people have said, 'Why can't you just be normal?'. I have always accepted that there is a misalignment between myself and the rest of the world. This, however, has never given me the feeling of being a lesser person; in fact it has always been the opposite. I have grown up with the permanent frustration that the majority of people simply do not work correctly but that is the way of the world. While attempting to blend in I have developed an overconfidence in who I am. This belief has allowed me to survive disappointment, job sacking, relationship breakdown and social faux pas.

I have spent my life watching people, learning social norms and rules, imitating social manners and etiquette. I have learnt to be a successful salesman. There are rules to selling which centre around placing the other person in a position where they have no alternative but to buy. I have learned to suppress certain emotional reactions that when displayed have appeared to others childlike in their overanimation.

I have taken on a persona that is a combination of the fictitious characters James Bond and Bertie Wooster because both characters are funny, stylish and popular. Both characters have been special interests of mine since I was very young, and I have all their books and films. I have created a socially acceptable self and now survive as a fashionista – I love wearing unusual colourful fashionable clothing. I have developed a cool steely persona that cannot be hurt but is also very charming and funny and that by using self-deprecating humour where I am the object of ridicule I gain popularity.

The diagnosis explained why there had always been a misalignment and in a way set me free to be myself rather than emulating the reactions of others. I enjoy being the Bertie Wooster/James Bond character and would feel lost not having them as the blueprint to my life as this has also given me a love of England, culture, antiques and fine clothing.

For the past 20 years, I have used my neurotypical wife as a template or guide for social norm, rather than my juvenile excitable outbursts of emotion. I have noted that she never discusses her personal emotion or reveals them in an exuberant manner and feels that discussing them in public makes her vulnerable, and so I have adopted this. However, it has resulted in a burying of my emotions so deep it has taken me some intense effort to retrieve them again. In an attempt to understand the benefits of her working this way I have quizzed her relentlessly over the years. She has claimed that my relentless quizzing has made her depressed as she does not know why she works this way. I operate so differently to her in the sense that I am much more rational and less emotional. For example, she would get jealous if I was friendly with another woman, or she would want repeated reassurance that I love her. I just don't see the need – I have told her I love her on many occasions – why the need for such repetition?

To be honest our marriage has struggled particularly since my diagnosis, where she has become depressed and unhappy, saying, 'the person I married isn't the person I thought he was'. She says she wants me to 'get better and be normal', saying, 'you're too logical, not emotional enough', rather than accepting me for who I was. We are now separated at her request as she has found romance with somebody at her work whom she says is 'more empathic'. I have finally achieved the cathartic experience of crying, which I have enjoyed very much. Wallowing in sadness has been strangely satisfying; however, I am not able to dwell on these emotions for long as my strong logical brain kicks in and tells me that I have had enough and puts them away again.

Since our separation I have had to develop a social life away from my wife, and the freedom of the diagnosis has allowed me to revert back to the colourful character that I was 20 years ago. I have discovered that the majority of people find my gregarious overzealous nature refreshing and people are accepting of me when I explain that my exuberance is a result of the fact that my brain is wired up differently and that autism is not a thing to be feared.

I purposely seek out other autistic people and want to inspire them to believe in themselves, suggesting they have been gifted with an insight to do great things and explaining the advantages of being able to control how they feel with the power of their logical minds. Emotions have a purpose but in my view neurotypical people have emotions in abundance and are controlled by them. The diagnosis has set me free to be myself and not feel bad about it!

7 Melanie's story: 'It's validated me – I'm more autistic militant now'

The experience of getting a diagnosis has made me more autistic militant. Instead of hiding it and thinking that I'm just odd, I'm more likely to stand up for myself and my rights. I will enjoy my sensory sensitivities – things I really enjoy – like swimming in the river, standing with my toes in swishy mud, listening to the rustling of a tree, feeling the leather of the steering wheel of my car or rainbows and waterfalls. I will ask for a quiet table in a restaurant; I will tell somebody pushing against me and squashing into me on the tube to keep away; and I will flap my hands at work when I am stressed.

I had a disciplinary at work before the diagnosing, where they said I was 'bullying a colleague', but in my view I was just being honest, telling her straight, albeit I am a bit too blunt. Now I have told my fellow nurses at work: 'I've got Asperger's so I won't know if you're unhappy or cross unless you start crying or shouting, so you will have to tell me. If you see me being inappropriate or getting stressed just tell me.' The young nurses are great and just accept me and the situation, but the older ones can be a bit difficult. I know we all have to fit in and it is a compromise between the autistic world and the neurotypical world but I don't suppress or rein it as much. Before I used to think I was odd – as a child I used to think that I was a fairy child although my parents did not think so – now I feel validated and I'm happier being me.

My sister said 'that explains why you had temper tantrums when anyone sat in your chair at the table or you wouldn't wear wool or you'd go out in a summer dress in the snow in winter'.

8 Jennie's story: 'I still feel angry … I'll never catch up'

Wednesday, 1 October 2014, another date to add to my ever-growing collection of memorable/unforgettable dates. This date may offer an explanation as to why dates play such an important part in my life, why I remember every significant date. This is the date I was diagnosed with Asperger's syndrome.

The Asperger's diagnosis came as a surprise to me and my family. I initially refused an assessment, but it was eventually taken out of my hands when I was sectioned under the Mental Health Act. To be taken off the section I had to agree to be referred for an assessment.

I feel angry about having the diagnosis of Asperger's. I am angry that I now have a diagnosis that I don't know what to do with. I am angry that I'm angry. I don't like being angry; anger is something that terrifies me. I'm angry when people say, 'Albert Einstein had Asperger's', because I'm not Albert Einstein. I don't have any special talents; I'm not a genius; and I'm fed up of hearing about it.

My initial thoughts following the diagnosis were it must be wrong. I can't have Asperger's. This is still one of the most dominant feelings that I have. I am struggling to settle the diagnosis in my own mind. The more I read about Asperger's the more things make sense: my love of routine and order, my strong belief about right and wrong, my strong dislike of change, my social difficulties and sensitivity to touch. All of it fits, yet I can't seem to accept the diagnosis.

The diagnosis, though unwanted, has in a way provided a form of relief. It helps provide an explanation to some of my quirks, and also helps my friends and family understand parts of my sometimes strange behaviour.

I have always had strong thoughts about what I should achieve to become a successful and worthy person. I set myself targets to reach by certain birthdays – by age 25 I wanted to be in full-time employment, own my own car and be living independently. By age 30 I wanted to be in a relationship, progressing in my job and looking to buy my own home. Now at 29 all but one of the targets have been missed. I own my own car – my dream car. The Asperger's diagnosis has made me question whether I will ever be able to reach these targets. It has made me question whether I will ever be the person that I want to be. The diagnosis has made me realise that I need to re-evaluate my aims and reconstruct my hopes for the future. Before the diagnosis I had accepted/realised that I was different to my friends/peers, but a part of me had always thought I would catch up, at some point something would click. The diagnosis makes me feel like this is unlikely to ever happen – it has taken away some hope. It is unlikely that I will ever catch up or be the person I want to be.

Although the diagnosis may potentially answer some questions, it also raises a lot of new ones. Overall I still have very mixed feelings about the Asperger's diagnosis. Now I have had time to digest the diagnosis, I am able to see some positives and understand why it was important to have the assessment.

9 Max's story: 'I was a hermit ... Now I try and live in the real world'

My life was always quite challenging, but I thought I was OK in primary school, as I kept to my small group of friends from a small, close-knit housing estate where everyone knew each other and connections were easily built and maintained. All that changed when I started secondary school, which was a bus journey away, not a short walk down the road. I was torn away from my comfort zone and felt traumatised. Due to my quietness, I was put through a special needs class. I scored 100 per cent on their test, so they naively decided I didn't need any help. I was being picked on for almost everything, including being quiet, and mostly ended up sitting on my own. Eventually, my attendance dropped and I was only attending classes that interested me.

I attended college for a year studying music technology and got a distinction for my academic work. I specialised in Elvis Presley between 1953–56 – the period when he left school – signed for Sun Records and then signed for RCA in New York. I know all the records he made and who played on them. I tried to play guitar but was rubbish as I couldn't play with the other members of the group – I was out of sync, couldn't interact with them and was told my guitar playing was 'robotic'.

I dropped out of college and became a hermit for a couple of years. I would never leave the house, staying in my bedroom, usually with the curtains drawn. I grew my hair and nails and really didn't look after myself. My interests were also quite narrow; I loved my music and video games and would become obsessed with the story and the characters. I even built websites dedicated to my favourites. I made friends on the internet because I could join message boards dedicated to subjects I was interested in. Writing is so much easier than speaking.

Eventually, I pushed myself out of the house, to meet a girl that I'd met online. Playing video games was good, but I craved human interaction outside. I fell in love with Mandy and soon moved in with her and her parents. She had everything in common with me, so it was much easier to connect with her. Even better, we had broken the ice on the internet, so I didn't have to suffer with any of the small talk. However, I was extremely uncomfortable with her family and would hide away in her room in the day when she went to work.

I had always suspected I had Asperger's syndrome and eventually reached the breaking point where I had to get help to find out if my suspicions were correct.

I eventually got an appointment to see a psychologist. I was absolutely terrified, but after a few hours, I was diagnosed. I was so happy; I finally understood why I had acted this way all of my life. It was liberating. A few months later, I was invited along to a few support sessions, where I was able to meet other adults who had also been diagnosed with Asperger's syndrome. We all sat in a waiting room, and it was actually great to see people tapping their feet, biting their nails and flapping their hands and fingers. It was great to see people who acted the same way I did and felt the same way I did in these situations – I was not alone.

The diagnosis did change my life. I am more comfortable in myself because I know the reason why I act certain ways. Mandy accepted my diagnosis and has been very supportive – I think she is a little bit 'on the spectrum' herself. We have our own flat now and I have a job as a cleaner, which I really enjoy. I'm good at it because I like the routine, regularity and structure and I'm on my own. I only wish that my condition had been spotted earlier on in life, as I might have got help in school and wouldn't have spent all those years in my bedroom as a hermit.

Being in the real world is my main difficulty. I am fine on my own or with Mandy, but if I go on a train or in a coffee shop I have my iPod on or wear my sunglasses. I know I have got to get a balance between being in the real world and being in my own world. If I go into a coffee shop I try not to wear my ipod all the time and try to make some small talk with the person serving rather than just saying 'cappuccino please'.

10 Julia's story: 'If I had known earlier I might have saved my job'

It is frightening when you feel different and I've always felt different, almost as if I spoke a different language to everybody else. As a child I'd say things wrong and I'd have no idea what I'd done – I had a complete blind spot. I am unaware of how I appear to others because it's difficult to see things from their point of view. I just saw people recoiling from me. Friendships were a struggle to initiate and maintain.

I always knew the issue lay with me as I just didn't know what to say. It's like everybody else seemed to 'know'; they had a handbook or script and I hadn't been given one. I have got better over the years and one key turning point was practising smiling and saying hello when greeting people.

The diagnosis was an epiphany, a turning point in my life and answered about 50 years' worth of questions. Afterwards I spent a lot of time reinterpreting things that had happened to me, with a lot of 'if only' regrets. Suddenly there was an explanation for the gaffes and misunderstandings over the years. I have wounds and deep scars inflicted by people as they have reacted to my autism. All the unpleasantness can now be put down to something other than my flawed moral character. I am not a bad person after all – it wasn't my fault. Many people whom I have known over the years – work colleagues, parents and siblings have formed an opinion about me which has not always been complimentary. It is difficult to explain to them that I do have a problem, but it's not what they thought it was.

I started to meet with other Aspies and really did feel at home for the first time – I felt included and accepted by that group. We would share our common experiences and there was a lot of head nodding and reassurance. We are all very different and don't conform to any stereotype, but underneath there is something that we all have in common.

Perhaps my greatest regret is that I didn't follow up my initial encounter with the concept of Asperger's syndrome, which was mentioned in an article in 'New Scientist' in April 2001. The article, by Professor Simon Baron-Cohen, proposed a list of 10 questions, and invited anyone who could answer 'yes' to all 10 to write in and take part in his research. I scored 8 and 2 possibles. I didn't take it any further at the time because I worried that if I took the article to my GP, he would just say stop wasting time.

In 2011, I was made redundant from my job as an engineer and feel that if I'd have had the diagnosis then I might have done better at work and saved my career. Unfortunately I got a diagnosis a year after losing my job. They were making redundancies and I was told 'you don't fit in', which was probably right, but very upsetting to hear. I know that I was one of the better engineers and always got on with the job and produced good work, but I didn't have any allies or friends at work. I couldn't do superficial small talk and my direct, rather blunt, but always honest manner put me on the wrong side of office politics.

I used to get angry if people interrupted me after I'd said a few words, thinking they knew what I meant, but in fact they didn't and they'd take the conversation off in a direction I didn't intend and I'd have to drag it back again. Or they would 'interpret' what I said, drawing inferences, which again I didn't intend. I have a deep need to work out how the world works, so I end up asking questions – too many questions. I want to understand things. I am very intolerant of ambiguity and if things are not clear it feels as if everything is going to fall apart. Having the diagnosis means that I have legal rights and have a legal disability which means I would have been entitled to 'reasonable adjustments' in the workplace and maybe I'd still be there today.

I am very glad that I got the diagnosis as it has been a great help – knowing that my difficulties have a biological basis makes them much easier to deal with. I carry a card around in my wallet in case I get into difficult situations. The message says something like, 'Please don't take it personally if my behaviour seems odd; I'm autistic and don't express myself very well in unfamiliar situations.'

Although initially I was relieved, my feelings gradually changed and I became angrier that I wasn't diagnosed earlier and there was a sense of frustration at being misunderstood for much of my life. But I'd much rather be angry than confused and depressed!

Chapter Five

Cognition, thinking and learning

1 Introduction – unusual profiles

People with autism often have an uneven, unusual profile of cognitive or intellectual functioning. In some areas the person might be significantly above average, even exceptional and very poor or below average in other areas. This diversity means that it is sensible to exercise extreme caution when making generalisations or talking about concepts such as overall intelligence. Occasionally, school pupils with this uneven profile of academic abilities are misdiagnosed as having a learning disability, when in fact this is not the case. For example, people with AS often have a great talent and interest in identifying perceptual patterns and sequences and score above average on psychometric tests, such as *Progressive Matrices*, where the subject has to identify which pattern matches a more complex pattern, or *The Block Design*, where the subject has to construct designs using coloured blocks. On the contrary, people with AS often have slow information processing, possibly due to their tendency to notice patterns and details or it might be that they are processing information in one channel rather than multiple channels. Autistic intelligence is different and problems arise when people try to compare it with more conventional, academic types of intelligence measured in schools.

2 Attention

There are three types of attention: (1) sustained attention, which means concentrating on one thing for a long period of time; (2) divided or split attention, which means concentrating on two things at the same time; and (3) switching attention, meaning, switching attention backwards and forwards between different items or stimuli. People with AS are often remarkably good at sustained attention, but not so good at divided attention or switching attention. However, this sustained attention and ability to process information depends on how the information is presented. People with AS are often superior at processing information if it is static, concrete, factual details, presented sequentially, but less good at processing dynamic, multiple simultaneously presented information.

As outlined in the weak central coherence theory, people with AS are remarkably good at attending to detail, having an 'eagle eye' for spotting details they are interested in. This single-channel, monoprocessing is strength for situations of sustained attention, but becomes a weakness for being able to stand back and perceive and understand the overall picture. It's as if people with AS are looking at the world through a rolled-up piece of paper, being unable to see the wider picture. Sometimes people are able to concentrate or sustain attention for considerable time almost in a trance-like state, oblivious to external stimulation. Nick was a computer coder/programmer and said: 'I can hyperfocus and sometimes spend 10 hours a day working on a piece of code without taking a break for food or drink. I don't notice my body or anything around me. Afterwards I'm exhausted and need to sleep.' However, if the person with AS is not interested in the subject, they often have a problem filtering out extraneous background stimulation or information and are therefore easily distracted.

A common difficulty is with joint or divided and switching attention or attending to multiple cues. Frequently people with AS will say,

- I find it difficult to look at you and talk at the same time.
- I find it difficult to listen and take notes at the same time, in a lecture.
- I'm not very good at thinking and talking at the same time.
- I don't like subtitled films because I have to read, look and listen all at once.

This is the same problem that the autistic baby has with looking at what a parent is pointing to. This skill involves the ability to monitor the gaze of another while following the direction of their pointing finger, looking to what is pointed at and then looking back to the gaze of the pointer. Switching attention is also a common problem and it is as if the person with AS becomes so 'locked on to' one thing they struggle to change gear or be flexible enough to switch to something else. The AS thinking style is a one-track mind. Alex commented:

> I'm so bad at multitasking that when I'm watching TV, I completely zone out of everything else. If the phone rings I don't hear it. If my flat mate comes into my room to give me a message they have to stand in front of the TV before I realise they're saying something to me! People get so cross but I can't help it. I really don't like being interrupted, because then I feel I have to start again.

3 Executive functioning

People with AS are generally not good at tasks that involve the 'big picture' or 'executive skills'. To fully understand what 'executive skills' are think of all the tasks that the chief executive of a large organisation does.

- Seeing the overall picture – taking a perspective.
- Multitasking by switching and dividing attention.
- Planning and organising – thinking ahead, imagining the future..
- Setting goals and organising ways to achieve those goals.
- Recognising mistakes and modifying plans if necessary.
- Prioritising what is most important.
- Problem solving and 'abstract reasoning'.
- Making decisions.
- Being aware of the details but not getting sucked in by them.
- Managing time successfully.

People with AS often struggle in roles that involve executive functioning and are much better as backroom technicians who are left to work on a particular project that involves detailed attention in one particular area. Executive skills as described are located in the frontal lobes of the brain, and human beings have large well-developed frontal lobes unlike animals further down the evolutionary scale. It could be argued that human civilisation has expanded at the same rate as mankind's frontal lobes have evolved. People with AS are not good at psychometric tests such as the *'Wisconsin Card Sorting Test,'* which involves holding in mind a number of tasks at the same time, switching attention, while at the same time trying to work out what is going on, given that the instructions to carry out the task are deliberately vague.

Felicity was a client of mine, who stands out as one of the best examples of somebody with poor executive skills, but a great eye for detail. She was 18 years old when initially referred by a psychiatrist who had diagnosed her with depression. Felicity wasn't really depressed but was highly anxious and had undiagnosed AS. She was highly intelligent and got four *A**s for her A levels and had been accepted to study at Cambridge University. Her mother and I anticipated numerous social problems, sensory problems and difficulties with changed routine, and wrote various letters to the university special needs department, her tutor and mentor, who all made various allowances. She had a special quiet en suite room, which she did not have to vacate in holiday times like the other students, and was even allowed to take her pet iguana. However, two problems arose that we didn't anticipate. One was that in the first year Felicity had great difficulty finding her way from her room to the lecture theatre block, which was a short walk along the ancient paved stoned streets of Cambridge. Her sense of direction was extremely poor and she would often get lost. When asked how she tried to remember the route, she commented, 'I will look at the cracks in the paving stones, or count the paving stones, and look out for the daffodils'. I asked, 'What if the daffodils were out of season?', to which she replied, 'I'd still be able to see the stalks'. Felicity was great on the small miniscule detail but not very good at standing back and perceiving the overall picture or holding in mind a mental map of the streets of Cambridge.

A second, similar problem was that Felicity struggled with writing academic essays, where there was a need to map out the answer, stand back, make a plan, make decisions about what was important, what was a detail, give opinions and a coherent argument. She could remember and regurgitate individual fact after fact, which is why she had done so well at A level, but she wasn't very good at making abstract connections, identifying what were the main ideas and minor details, making summaries, metaphysically hovering over the project and seeing the overall picture – like a helicopter hovering over a landscape so the pilot is able to see the lie of the land. Felicity invariably got sucked into the details, literally had her nose to the ground looking at the cracks in the pavement and getting lost, and in her essays getting tied up in facts and small details. The ability to write a university essay requires a different style of thinking – executive thinking – than the thinking required at school.

It turned out that Felicity's devoted mother ended up being her 'executive secretary', helping her plan and organise her university essays. In essence her mother was taking on the function of Felicity's frontal lobes, making suggestions, prompting, doing the thinking, linking, summarising, decision making, prioritising and helping her to change track when necessary. Mum often had to correct and redirect Felicity if she was using the wrong strategy on an essay as she seemed to struggle to learn from here mistakes. People with AS often perform better if given external support, someone to give a reminder, a direction or create some structure. It is almost as if people with AS are not good at spontaneously using the full range of mental skills that they have – their underlying executive skills can be dormant – and often need a prompt to 'boot up' those skills .

Felicity also had a problem with remembering faces (prosoagnosia) and often remembered people by a detail such as their hair. Her mother related a story about picking Felicity up from school one day after having had a haircut and Felicity not recognising her in the school playground, being unable to pick her out from the other mothers because of the change in appearance. I'm glad to say that with a great deal of support, Felicity eventually obtained her degree.

Another executive functioning with which people with AS often have a problem is time perception. Awareness of the time is partially an executive skill, because it involves holding in mind that thread of what the time is approximately, while at the same time getting on with the day's activities. It is another aspect of multitasking and dividing attention, which sometimes is difficult for the person with AS who is more inclined to have a one-track mind. The person with AS can sometimes be ,'lost in a sea of time'. This may mean that planning ahead, which involves imagination and thinking in terms of the future, is problematic. This can make situations such as examinations particularly difficult as the person cannot work out how long to spend on each question. Nigel illustrates this point:

> In my job as a cleaner I have to be given a breakdown of the specific tasks I have to do in the day as well as an allocated amount of time to spend on each task. I then set my phone alarm to go off and alert me when it's time to switch tasks. Without this I would be oblivious to the time and spend too long on each task making sure it was perfect and not getting round to completing all the jobs on the list. Before I started using my phone as a prompt to switch tasks I used to be there all evening, working hours I wasn't paid for.

Decision making is another executive skills task where many people with AS have difficulty. Again, part of the problem is getting sucked into the detail and not being able to stand back, weigh things up and see what is important. Decisions are also often made by a 'gut reaction' or emotional response which tips the balance in one direction. A strong emotional pull is often lacking in people with AS, which leaves the person struggling with a huge amount of detailed information that they find difficult to parcel up. It also does not help if the person is something of a perfectionist and have a strong desire to 'get it right' or not 'make the wrong decision'. Making a decision usually means excluding alternatives and other options. This type of perfectionism can often paralyze the person into inactivity. Jennie's story illustrates this:

> I don't do decision making. I hate making decisions about what to wear, so I just always wear black – usually the same clothes. It's much easier. I've also got a box full of birthday cards because in the shop I can't decide which one to buy and end up buying three or four and making my mind up when I get home. Christmas is difficult because there are so many decisions to make. If I buy a car I have to do a massive analysis, looking at all the facts, specifications and comparison sites – it's a nightmare. I wish I could just go into a car showroom and say, 'Ooh I love that red one, I'll have it'.

4 Memory

Generally, people with AS perform well on tests which require the ability to learn and remember factual information (semantic memory) and are good at learning how to do things (procedural memory). Their minds are often like sponges, absorbing new facts and filling up categories and systems like an encyclopaedia. For example, they might be good at remembering the date the Magna Carta was signed, how an engine works or telephone numbers, postcodes and passwords. A person with AS, or AS traits, would be a real bonus in a quiz team.

However, people with AS often have poor autobiographical memories, or memories about their own personal experiences. The person might remember 'facts' or semantic information but are less likely to remember the feelings associated with events. The memory is often there but doesn't come spontaneously and the person might need prompting to recall a particular event. This might appear a small glitch in memory function but can contribute to a lack of sense of self and identity. People with AS sometimes don't get that 'carry over' from the past that gives a person a sense of self. Often the person has an extensive vocabulary, with a detailed knowledge of the meaning of words, and how to pronounce the word correctly. Sometimes the AS person might even have a photographic memory with the ability to accurately recall scenes or whole pages of book. Pupils with AS are sometimes wrongly accused of cheating in exams because they can reproduce, almost exactly, long pages of text from textbooks. One young man, Jermaine, was criticised by his teacher for not writing careful notes to study for his examination. He commented:

> I didn't write notes like everybody else partly because my handwriting was so poor, but also because I didn't need to, as I could remember everything without writing it down. I could visualise all the information from the text book. My teacher would be constantly criticising me and moaning to my parents, but in the end I got an *A** in the exam.

For most of us though this is not a recommended study technique! However, paradoxically, even though people with AS might have an excellent rote memory for learning and storing information, they can very often be forgetful when it comes to remembering to do things in the future. This is a slightly different type of memory called 'prospective memory', which involves holding something in mind, to do in the future (eg I must ring my mother this evening), while at the same time getting on with everyday life. This type of memory is linked to executive functioning, multitasking and skills associated with the frontal lobes of the brain. An aspect of memory called 'working memory' is also a weakness for people with AS. This is the ability to hold in mind a piece of information very briefly, holding in temporary store for a few seconds.

Less than 10 per cent of people with autism have 'a degree of savant skill' or a photographic memory, with an exceptional ability to recall details. Synder (2012) suggests this savant-like state is a pure form of autism, a mind that builds from parts to a whole, gets sucked into detail, has weak central coherence and limited ToM. There are people like the artistic Steven Wiltshire, creator of photorealistic cityscapes, who can remember all the details, including all the windows and turrets, of the Houses of Parliament, with one flight past in a helicopter and reproduce it in a highly detailed drawing. Synder's theory is that there is an atypical hemisphere imbalance or brain dysfunction in the left anterior temporal lobe, which is being compensated for by right hemisphere's visual and spatial skills. Synder suggests that the left anterior temporal lobe is responsible for concept formation, packaging and labelling, assembling unprocessed raw information into wholes or holistic labels. If that area is damaged, either by a physical injury, a dementia (of the fronto-temporal type) or left hemisphere stroke, these savant-like skills can appear or be released. It is as if the poorly functioning left hemisphere allows the right hemisphere, with its visual and perceptual skills, to be enhanced and take centre stage. Skills associated with savant-like abilities include having perfect pitch, hyperlexia and precocious reading ability as a young child.

Synder's research has shown that savant like skills can be artificially induced by repetitive transcranial magnetic stimulation, creating a virtual lesion, resulting in these savant-like skills being unleashed. People's drawing styles become more detailed; proofreading skills can improve; and numerosity, the ability to accurately guess large number of objects, are enhanced. The picture which emerges is that these savant like skills, where there is a great attention to detail, are being 'suppressed' by 'higher processing' which bundles up the details into concepts, wholes and packages. If we switch off the higher functioning savant like skills appear. Unfortunately, this research has only a limited evidence base and has not been replicated in other centres. There is also some suggestion that as social and communication skills improve, with age, these pure 'savant' like skills diminish.

Marita, a young lady who was training to be a doctor, related a telling story.

> I have a photographic memory. I can remember every day of my life and can tell you what I was wearing and what I was eating and what I did and where I sat – it's very annoying. If I read a sign walking around a National Trust property I can't help but memorise it. I've read all the Harry Potter books at least 10 times and have read Matilda over 80 times. I was sitting on a train staring into space re-reading the fifth Harry Potter book in my mind without the actual book and a lady opposite asked me what I was doing. I said, 'I'm reading Harry Potter' To which she said, 'But where's the book dear?'. My stupid memory is very useful in exams and was very good when I was a proofreader but it is really annoying! Strangely my memory for routes is awful and I struggle to find the way to the local supermarket.

5 Mathematics, reading and writing

About a quarter of children with AS are outstanding at mathematics and a quarter have real problems with it. Some have dyscalculia, which means they struggle to work out even the most basic mathematical concepts such as adding and subtracting or telling the time. Mathematics is a popular subject among people with AS because of the enjoyment of rules and certainty that are associated with calculations and tables and their strong eye for detail. If you know the correct answer you can prove it.

One client was particularly good at poker because he could work out the mathematical probabilities and also had a poker face which didn't show any emotion. One schoolgirl posed a puzzle to her teachers as she did have dyscalculia and couldn't do mathematics, couldn't tell the time and couldn't take 6 away from 10 but knew all her timestables. Why? Because she has a photographic savant type memory that recorded everything. So she could recall a picture in her mind, a memory of a times table, but that skill was very separate from the cognitive skill required to add, subtract and multiply. Rupert commented:

> I was always good at pure maths at school and would get 98 per cent in exams and an *A** at A level. But when I got to university I had to do something called abstract maths and I just couldn't do it. I got 2 per cent in one exam. They would ask you to do things like prove that 1 is greater than 0. I couldn't think or imagine how to do it. I'm great with maths when there is a formula, a structured problem to solve, all straight lines and black and white. But abstract maths – no thanks! I dropped the maths degree at the end of the first year.

The following poem, posted on the Tony Attwood, Asperger's website, captures well the understandable attraction between people with AS and numbers.

Numbers by David LeBlond

I like numbers
they just add and subtract
they don't hurt your feelings
or overreact
you can count on numbers
to make things work out
there's no second-guessing
no worry or doubt
numbers are my respite
my port in the storm

when the world is cruel and cold
they are safe and warm
now they're not much to look at
(although eight is not bad)
they don't make you love them
or make you be sad
one thing about numbers
that won't be denied
they play by the rules
you cannot hide
if you make a mistake
or forget where you're at
they just won't forgive you
... we need people for that

Poor handwriting is a common problem and is part of the dyspraxic area of difficulty associated with poor movement and fine motor coordination or bilateral coordination problems. To view the problem from a positive perspective and be innovative, it could be considered an obsolete skill, as people in the future will type or use voice activation software. If writing is not a strength, ask if an oral, rather than a written, report would be suitable.

At least one in five children with AS have significant problems with reading. There is a condition called hyperlexia which can occur with children on the autism spectrum, where they learn to read very quickly and precociously but actually don't understand the meaning of what they are reading. One man described being a child, and being able to read the newspapers fluently before starting school, but not really understanding what he was reading. There is often that 'eagle-eyed' attention to detail, combined with an exceptional memory, resulting in reading words correctly, but actually not having the ability to know the meaning of the sentences or the overall picture.

Chapter Six

Language

1 Using language socially – 'pragmatics'

Many children on the autism spectrum are late in their development of speech, but they usually talk fluently by the age of five. Sometimes parents report that speech is delayed, but when it does start it starts with formed words, several words together or even a formed sentence. Language skills improve over time and problems are overcome. For most adults with AS the language difficulties are not immediately obvious. However, there can be a number of problems using language that are subtle and difficult to identify.

In the area of language, many people with AS are very precise in their choice of words, having wide vocabularies, but still are not very good at communicating. This is because communication requires more than words in order to be effective. Communication requires an understanding of non-verbal behaviour, the hidden meaning behind words and reading between the lines. Professionals refer to the social use of language as 'pragmatics'. Communication requires at a basic level at least two people, a message to communicate, the ability to communicate and the ability to check that this message has been successfully received. Effective communication requires that this is done accurately, in a timely manner, is appropriate to context and that any communication breakdown is repaired, where necessary.

The skill of effective communication involves not only articulating one's own thoughts, but at the same time having an awareness of what the other person is thinking, feeling and saying and linking it all together. This requires multiple channels of attention to be processing information at the same time. It often does not require perfectly enunciated words, complete sentences and overly formal language, but gestures, facial expressions, grunts and an inarticulateness that conveys a message. Richard commented, 'Thinking and speech don't go together naturally for me. I struggle to think and speak at the same time', or on a similar theme, 'Do you want eye contact or a conversation? I can't do both.'

Speaking occurs in a social context and communication isn't just by the words that people choose. One client, Natasha, training to be a doctor, in a busy hospital, illustrated this point well:

> If I'm going to understand people they need to speak directly, clearly and specifically to me, rather than making inferences. I was in the nurses' station the other day, with five other people, and the matron said, 'someone's got to do that X-ray today and raised her eyebrows'. I really didn't know she was referring to me, so I didn't do the X-ray and got into trouble. Why didn't she just call me by name and tell me exactly and precisely what I had to do rather than having this mysterious code?

So much of our communication is indirect, implied by a look, a nod, a smile, a gesture, which is difficult for the person with AS to pick up.

2 Reciprocal – two-way – conversations

Smooth, reciprocal conversations are often difficult. Alex said, 'For me my conversations don't flow smoothly like a river, I find it difficult to get into a rhythm'. Duncan said, 'When I watch other people's conversation it is like a game of table tennis, with lots of backwards and forwards – I find that difficult to do'. People with AS often have problems knowing how to start a conversation, with an 'opener', often just launching into a subject with a statement or question. Sometimes they may have difficulties knowing how to end a conversation – not having an 'off-switch', but just having to finish what they needed to say irrespective of the effect on the listener. There may also be a tendency to make irrelevant comments, not know when to reply, change the topic or have a tendency to interrupt. There may be a lack of 'check out comments' such as 'What do you think about that' or 'Do you know what I mean', or 'really', or verbal and non-verbal reinforces such as 'Hmn', 'Yes' 'uhuh' or head nodding. There may be a tendency to jump from topic to topic with no obvious link or 'connecting comment' – tangential thinking – which within reason can be creative, but the speaker is failing to acknowledge the perspective of the listener. There may be an inability to alter language according to the social context or even appreciate the social context. For example, if somebody says, 'How are you today?' as you pass them in the corridor, the context requires a brief response with few details. In fact, it's just a way of saying hello; it's a trick question; the other person usually doesn't want a conversation; they just expect you to say, 'Fine thanks and yourself' and pass on. A tendency to interrupt is often due to the person having difficulty identifying the cues of when to start talking such as a momentary pause or the other person's body language. For some people with AS there is a strong desire to finish what they have started, without interruptions, irrespective of the other person's response.

Sometimes people with AS tend to speak in a monologue oblivious to reactions or needs of their audience. If it is a subject the person has a genuine enthusiasm for, words flow out garrulously, like a tap being turned on or like a 'babbling brook'. This can be worse if the person has poor eye contact unaware of the other person's reaction. It is almost as if they have found somebody to listen and now have the opportunity to talk, and talk they will. At the other extreme for some people speaking can be a torturous experience where words do not always come out and it is difficult to translate thoughts into words. Stuart found it difficult to talk spontaneously because he needed his thoughts to be perfectly formed before he would allow them to leave his mouth. A lack of variation in facial expression, rather flat, poor body language, with few gestures limits the person's ability to communicate. Felicity's mother commented, 'She didn't have a great range of facial expressions, rarely smiled, always had a serious face and was very much in her own world'.

Often the person with AS is unsure of what the other person wants and will either provide too much detailed information or too little.

The person might not be able to organise a 'narrative framework' or theme for disclosure and might provide too much detail and miss the point of the story or the punch line.

I asked one client how he had met his wife as they seemed a rather incongruous couple as the woman was an attractive, middle-class, well-spoken, university graduate with a career and he was a man with no educational qualifications, no job or career prospects and a tendency to ramble on about obscure technical subjects. 'I met Juliet when I was fixing her car. I ended up welding the floor of her Morris Minor which was in a shocking condition – really rusty. The camshaft had gone on ...' He then spent 10 minutes describing with great enthusiasm the inside of Juliet's engine and the mechanical specifications of the Morris Minor and completely missed the point of my question which was, 'Can you explain how you two people are together and have stayed together for 10 years, when you are obviously so very different?'. I did not want to know about the details of the car that she had 10 years ago!

3 Literal interpretation of language – implied meaning (semantics)

People with AS often interpret literally what other people say. For example, if someone says, 'get your finger out', which is a figure of speech meaning you had better start making more effort, they may start looking at their fingers. They are less aware of the hidden implied or multiple meaning in language, or idioms or metaphors. A good example of this is the story of the teacher who said to the autistic pupil, 'Don't worry; your mother is going to be late; she's tied up in the office.' The little boy immediately started screaming because he thought somebody had tied his mother up. I once said to a young lady recently diagnosed with AS, who had just obtained an 'Autism Alert Card', 'That's a useful thing to have up your sleeve.'

She was confused by the ambiguity of the metaphor, later saying on reflection, 'I don't understand about 10% of what people say, but I just nod and pretend I do. It's like people sometimes speak a different language.' The person with AS is often confused by teasing, joking, irony, innuendo or sarcasm and doesn't pick up the intentions or hidden meanings, having a tendency to make a literal interpretation. However, this is a skill that improves with age and is much less apparent in adults than in children.

Liane Holliday Willey (2015, p23) commented:

> As a child I took language and words very literally. Metaphors, similes and analogies did not exist to me. I never considered that the statement had more than one meaning. I was continually baffled unchallenged by what people said. My parents and teachers thought I was being obstinate disobedient audacious and pedantic ... I understood their language, knew if they made grammatical errors in their speech, but I never understood their vernacular. I was unable to read between the lines, subtexts, innuendoes to understand their thought processes of my peers.

Emma, a client of mine with AS, whom I was seeing for a few post-diagnostic counselling sessions, corrected me very firmly once after I had opened our therapy session with the comment, 'How are you?'. She replied in a rather frustrated manner, '"How are you" is not a real question; it is a vagary. It doesn't mean anything. It's just annoying when people say that. Why don't you say something more accurate and precise such as, "To what degree has your mood fluctuated over the last week?"'.

4 Difficulty with prosody – the melody, tone and rhythm of speech

An important part of communication in a conversation is our ability to change vocal tone, volume, to emphasise certain words, to add emotion and vary pitch. For some people with AS, there is a lack of variation in rhythm, pitch and stress or melody of speech which leaves the speech with a rather flat monotonous quality. For some people, their speech is slightly too loud or has a high-pitched or nasal quality and does not convey the amount of social and emotional information that enrich their language. Some children with AS have had training and advice from speech and language therapists on how to improve their prosody by using the kind of techniques that actors use. They learn the relevance of a change of tone or emphasis in someone else's conversation and how to do this themselves.

5 Pedantic or too formal speech

Sometimes adults with AS may be overly formal and pedantic and precise in their speech. As children their speech is often too 'adult' or correct, and instead of saying, 'Mum said don't do that', they might say, "My mother said I should not do that'. They use correct English but sacrifice meaning and expression. Speech is overprecise and ponderous. One man said: 'I am acutely sensitive to words and can be quite obsessive. I obsess about whether one word is better than another to express my thoughts, which takes a long time. The teacher at school would get annoyed over my writing and talking.' Another one said: 'I'm a grammar Nazi and get caught up in insignificant detail whether people use "is" when it should be "are" "of" instead of "off", or their use of modal verbs or apostrophes really annoys me.' They might correct other people's speech, which can be annoying as they have to be precise and can't take a shortcut, can't walk across the grass if the sign says 'don't'. Liane Holliday Willey said, 'Language appeals to me because it lends itself to rules and precision' (p38). Pedantic language usually implies giving too much correct information, too much detail, but can also mean not giving enough information. Again there is a lack of awareness of what the other person needs.

6 Sensory language and neologisms

In the past, autistic people with no or poor language skills were diagnosed as mentally retarded and sent to institutions, but now we know that often they have a form of autistic intelligence that is simply not based on words and language. When we are babies, our world comprises sensory input and images, but we gradually acquire the use of language – there is a gradual transition from the sensory to verbal. This is the same for people with autism but the transition is often slower and more difficult and sometimes doesn't happen at all, resulting in what is known as 'autistic muteness'. But people without language can still communicate, although their language is based on sensory impressions, sounds, touch, smells and images. Tito, a man diagnosed with autism, said, 'Words have no meaning; they are just noises like a dog barking'. Richard explained: 'My first language is sensory, non-verbal. Every time I use a word, I'm using my second language. It's like I'm bilingual. I learned to speak by listening to the radio. That's why I sound like a Radio Four presenter.' This explains why sometimes people with AS will make up or invent idiosyncratic words (neologisms). These are often words that have a sensory onomatopoeic association with the object, such as 'clink' for a magnet, 'pinklipstar' for lipstick or 'foosh' for cat.

Chapter Seven

Sensory sensitivity and motor coordination

1 Types of sensory sensitivity

Over the past few decades, clinicians have become more aware of the problem of sensory sensitivities in people with autism, confirmation of this being that 'sensory issues' are now a key symptom in the diagnostic manual DSM-5. For some people with AS, 'sensory sensitivity' or 'sensory integration difficulties' have a greater negative impact on their lives than problems that are created with the social and emotional world. Recent research found that over 80 per cent of an AS sample reported extreme levels of sensory processing in at least one way (Smith Myles et al, 2000). Sensations are perceived as unbearably intense and intolerable (oversensitive or hypersensitive); there is an absence of sensation (undersensitive or hyposensitive) or a difficulty filtering out sensations, in the following senses:

- auditory (Hearing, sound, noise)
- visual (sight, light, colour)
- olfactory (Smell)
- tactile (Touch, pain, temperature)
- gustatory (Taste, hunger)
- vestibular (movement, balance)
- proprioception (Awareness of body in space).

Many people would grimace at the sensation of nails being scratched down a blackboard, but imagine what it would be like if your hearing was hypersensitive and that reaction occurred for you in many situations. Temple Grandin (1995) commented: 'Loud noises hurt my ears like a dentist drill hitting a nerve ... for others touch can be painful – like razors drawn across the skin ... the ringing of the school bell always hurt my ears' (p81); 'As a baby I resisted being touched and when I became a little older I can remember stiffening, flinching and pulling away from relatives when they hugged me' (p155). When living with a mixture of these sensitivities, the world can become a threatening place, with the possibility of a dangerous environment around every corner.

Charlotte recalled her schooldays as being painful memories because of her sensory issues:

> At school, the dining room, playground and corridors were a constant insult to my senses as they were so noisy, coupled with the fluorescent lights, bells ringing and people bumping into each other. Then there was the smell of different cleaning products and peoples' scent and perfumes. Going to school was a nightmare. I can only describe it as like being in the jungle where around every corner there was an impending danger or if you imagine what it would be like to be stuck in a giant spin drier. Afterwards I'd feel really tired or drained.

Children with sensory sensitivity can become hypervigilant, tense and destructive in a sensory-stimulating environment such as the classroom, feeling unsure where the next painful sensory experience lurks.

We do not have a full understanding of the roots of these difficulties, but we know it is a neurological problem concerned with the way the brain processes and analyses information from our receptive sense organs, such as the ears, eyes, nose or tongue and skin and stomach. Our sense organs transform sensory stimuli (light, sound, odour etc) into electrical and chemical signals, which are identified, parcelled together and interpreted by the brain. Most of this sensory information (except smell) passes through the Thalamus and then to the opposite hemisphere of the cortex for further processing.

Many people with AS have difficulty processing sensory input for more than one sense at a time. The term often used to describe this is 'monotropic', or single channelled, which means struggling to multiprocess. The mono-processor has all the information gathered in one place, one sense, whereas the multiprocessor uses senses simultaneously, so when they are hearing something they will be aware of what they see, feel emotionally and physically. This appears most common in the auditory and visual pathways and may explain why some individuals struggle to look at other people when they are

Table 1: Hypersensitive versus hyposensitive

Sensory modality	Hypersensitive (heightened)	Hyposensitive (diminished)
Sight	Problem with bright (sunlight) or fluorescent lights. Pleasure in focusing on the details. Finding places with lots of visual stimulation overwhelming (supermarkets).	Poor depth perception resulting in problems with throwing or catching a ball.
Sound	Distressed by loud, high-pitched or sudden noises. Noises can be magnified or distorted. Can hear and are distressed by sounds that others don't notice. Difficulty filtering out distracting background noises.	May not hear or acknowledge particular sounds – can't hear one voice among others.
Touch	Dislike being touched, particularly light touch which can be painful. Dislike certain textures such as wool. Being very aware of temperature changes or strongly dislike being too hot or too cold.	Unaware of cuts or bruises. High pain threshold. Enjoy weighted objects on top of them.
Taste	Sensitive to tastes and textures mixing as the experience becomes too overwhelming. Often become fussy eaters where certain foods cannot be eaten together.	Limited or no awareness of appetite.
Smell	Certain smells become overpowering and too intense. May dislike people using perfume and aftershave and strong smelling flowers. Some people have such a sensitivity they can differentiate particular smells with exceptional accuracy.	Some have no sense of smell.

(***Continued***)

Table 1: Hypersensitive versus hyposensitive (*Continued*)

Sensory modality	Hypersensitive (heightened)	Hyposensitive (diminished)
Balance ('vestibular')	Situated in inner ear. Difficulty with sports where controlled movement and coordination are necessary. Car sickness.	Need to rock or spin to get some sensory input.
Body awareness ('proprio-ception')	Difficulty with fine motor skills: manipulating small objects like buttons or shoelaces.	Clumsy, may bump into people. Stand too close to people as cannot judge personal space. No sense of body temperature – don't feel the cold.

having a conversation and listening to them. Fay said: 'When I was a child, people would say "Look at me when I'm talking to you", but I found it distracting and overloaded my senses. My ideal position to talk to somebody would be sitting back to back or sitting alongside somebody who is in the passenger seat of a car.'

A further problem is the inability to filter out foreground and background information, to focus on what is selected and ignore the rest. Some people with AS seem to have no sieve in their brains to select information and filter out what is not worth attending to. A combination of these two factors – being single channelled and not having a filter – means that people with AS are often bombarded with information from simultaneous sources and are vulnerable to sensory overload.

2 Auditory or sound sensitivity

The most common sensitivity is to sound, which might be (1) a sudden unexpected noise like a dog barking, an alarm going off, a bell or a

Auditory sensory problem	Coping strategies
Find it hard to focus on what somebody is saying because you are distracted by other noises like a ticking clock, fan or light buzzing.	Turn off or remove background noise if possible. Go to a quiet place when you really need to focus. Use headphones to block out background noise.
Find loud noise bothersome and even sometimes painful.	Use noise cancelling earplugs, such as those used at loud concerts, which allow you to hear pertinent information but reduce the overall noise level.
Notice that you hear things that others don't notice.	Either remove the stimulus or try to mask it with calming repetitive sounds or music.

balloon bursting; (2) high-pitched continuous noises, for example, from an electric motor or vacuum cleaner; and (3) confusing, mixed, overlapping noises such as the cacophony in a shopping centre, busy restaurant or a school playground. There might also be a sensitivity to noise that other people don't notice such as a ticking clock. Some people with AS are so sensitive to sound and differentiating sounds that they have 'perfect pitch' and become expert musicians.

3 Visual or light sensitivity

Sensitivity to bright lights, such as mid-day sunlight or particular types of lighting such as a fluorescent lights or flickering light, can be troubling. One man said he was 'blinded by brightness'. Occasionally, there might be sensitivity to a particular colour. One woman said that she couldn't stand anything that was red. There can also be an intense fascination with certain visual details such as noticing a pattern on a carpet or a tiny scrap of paper on a floor.

Visual sensory problem	Coping strategies
Being unable to tolerate certain types of lighting such as fluorescent lights or a strong light or bright sunlight.	Change lighting, use lamps or low-watt bulbs or take breaks away from harsh lighting. Wear dark glasses or a hat to reduce glare from sunlight.
Finding places with a great deal of visual information overwhelming such as supermarkets.	Avoid shopping in large busy stores, or shop at quieter times. Take your glasses off so you can't see as clearly. Wear sunglasses or use lens with a coloured filter.
Being disorientated, dizzy or unable to relax in certain decorative environments.	Create calming spaces with limited visual input in your home. Have blank walls if necessary.
Being unable to find items in a busy environment.	Create systems, use filing cabinets, use clear labels so things stand out.

4 Tactile or touch sensitivity

Many people with AS cut the labels out of clothes because they are distressed by the sensation; others avoid scratchy material against the skin, such as wool. Some people don't like being touched and find the deep pressure of being squeezed more bearable than a light touch. Deborah Lipsky, who has AS herself, writes in her book *From Anxiety to Meltdown* (2011) of the similarity between some people with AS and herd animals, such as deer, cattle and horses – she owns an animal rescue centre. Lipsky notes both people with AS and herd animals have hypervigilant senses, a startle response to light touch and an aversion to direct eye contact. A horse touched very lightly will tend to react with a startle. Both find light contact unsettling and perceive direct eye contact to be threatening. Lipsky suggests that this is why people with AS might communicate and bond so well with animals. Lipsky also suggests that, for her, sensory overstimulation

Tactile sensory problem	Coping strategies
Find the feel of certain clothes or clothes' labels unpleasant and struggle to tune this out.	Choose clothes that you like the feel of. Cut out the labels. Wear an undervest.
Find light touch from others particularly troubling and need to take time to calm down afterwards.	Inform that you don't like it and that you would prefer deep pressure or a squeeze. Try a weighted blanket or tight body warmer.
Find personal grooming activities such as shaving, brushing teeth or cutting hair difficult.	Try different hairdressers, shaving kits or toothbrushes until you find the least noxious. Wear a hat if your hair becomes unruly.
Strongly dislike being too hot or cold and are very aware of any temperature changes.	Be more aware of your environment and choice of clothing.

does not respond to desensitisation as a treatment, suggesting that it is only the removal of the stimulus that works. She is of the opinion that these sensitivities are an inbuilt hardwired response: 'I tried to get used to clothing tags or labels on the back of my shirt, but couldn't. I tried convincing myself that I was overreacting and tried to desensitise myself, but my body overrode my mind ... I ended up running into the bedroom, grabbing the scissors and cutting out the offending tags.' Although desensitisation treatments may not be an ultimate cure, they can improve tolerance by increasing the AS person's threshold for arousal.

5 Olfactory or smell sensitivity

Some people with AS have very strong likes and dislikes for certain smells, finding certain aromas overpowering and intense. Common smells disliked include perfumes, deodorants, scents, chemicals in paints and disinfectants. One of my clients, Paulo, a successful Italian

Smell sensory problem	Coping strategies
Aversion to certain smells or someone wearing perfume or aftershave	Breath in through your mouth rather than nose. Carry an alternative favourite smell that is soothing. Let people know you have a smell sensitivity.
'I can't wear perfume; it gives me a headache'; aversion to some cleaning and bathing products	Don't wear it. Buy non-scented cleaning and bathing products.

IT consultant, told the story of how his sensory difficulties created problems for his love life:

> For some reason I am quite successful with women but I have to tell them I do not like light touch, preferring to be squeezed. On one occasion a girl turned up, whom I had met for the first time reeking of really strong perfume. I just had to say, 'Your smell is really too strong, could you please have a shower before we start talking, otherwise I will not be able to concentrate for the whole evening'. She wasn't very happy but complied and we had a nice evening.

On the positive side, one client's sensitivity to smell helped her greatly in developing a career as a perfume maker.

6 Taste sensitivity

Sensitivity to taste and texture of food is also fairly common and often results in people becoming extremely fussy eaters. Jake said:

> I can't have foods mixed up on a plate and I can't stand food being covered with a sauce. I eat each food separately. Why would you want to mix the taste of a carrot with meat? I am also supersensitive to anything that has a slimy texture and prefer food that is dry and, for example, always eat my cereal dry without milk.

Many adults with AS have quite a restricted diet often eating the same food for breakfast , lunch and dinner throughout their lives. As

Taste sensory problem	Coping strategies
Strong dislike of various tastes and texture of food	Try to strike a balance between following your preferences, expanding your range and mixing similar foods (eg carrots and peas). Try to desensitise yourself while relaxed.
Dislike of slimy food	Try mixing up slimy sensations by adding crunchy food such as celery or nuts.

long as the person has the right nutritional ingredients, this might not be a problem. But this is an area where people can attempt to be more flexible in a graduated way, trying to systematically desensitise themselves to different and varied foods. This desensitisation approach means very gradually, in stages, trying to expose themselves to an aversive food, initially just touching it, then maybe licking it, and finally maybe putting it in their mouth and swallowing it.

7 Other sensitivities to bodily states: Temperature, pain, hunger

Occasionally, a person will have a lack of sensitivity or awareness of bodily states such as hunger. One mother said, 'I didn't realise Ellie didn't know when she was hungry or not until one day when she was about six years old, I said "Are you hungry?" to which she replied, "how would I know"'. In Ellie's situation, there is a lack of connectivity between the appetite centre in the brain and the frontal thinking awareness part of the brain, and so the message that the body was hungry simply didn't get through. A similar lack of connectivity might occur in other situations, for example, when the child isn't aware of being cold, hot or in pain or discomfort. Some people have very high tolerance of pain and are not aware of life-threatening injuries or illnesses, which may result in the person putting themselves into risky situations or more frequent trips to the hospital. Having to cope with these extreme sensory experiences means people with AS sometimes appear very stoical, not flinching or showing distress, in response to pain that others that would consider unbearable. This characteristic is a useful trait to have for people who engage in extreme endurance sports. But if these signals that alert the person to danger are absent they might be more prone to injury.

8 Sensory overload, meltdowns and coping

An accumulation of sensory stresses, combined with other life stresses, including stress associated with socialising, can sometimes lead to overload and 'meltdowns'. Tamzin commented:

> I flipped, flew into a rage the moment my sensory system became overloaded. I call it 'brain fuzz, like a television being on the blink. I was already stressed at work. On top of that I've always hated the fluorescent lights; I was wearing a skirt I didn't really like and new shoes, which were uncomfortable. But what tipped me over the edge was when the fire alarm went off. It was only a practice but was just the final straw.

Temple Grandin invented a hug or squeeze machine after realising that deep pressure can reduce her hypersensitivity and the anxiety it causes. The idea for this device came when she noticed that the cattle being branded in a squeeze chute at her aunt's farm calmed down as soon as the pressure was administered. Grandin built her own machine for herself and could vary the pressure and time duration of the squeeze depending on her own needs. Liane Holliday Willey (2008, p30) describes having safety zones where she could get away from sensory overload, such as climbing into an alcove under her bed: 'Whenever things became too fuzzy, or loud or too distracting; whenever I began to feel as though I would become unravelled, I knew I could crawl into my alcove and crunch up into it, until I felt a square and symmetry. I could squeeze my knees and pull my thoughts back into my bones.'

Stephen found a useful assertive strategy by telling people that he had 'sensory integration problems', to explain his poor eye contact: 'I find it useful to say to people, "I just want you to know that although I'm looking down at the floor, I'm hearing every word you say". I have visual and auditory sensory integration difficulties that make sustaining eye contact difficult.'

9 General ways of coping with sensory sensitivities

(a) **Some sensitivities diminish with age but generally it is a lifelong condition**: Unfortunately we must accept that sensory issues tend not to go away, although there is evidence that suggests that they tend to diminish during adolescence (Attwood 2007, p290).

(b) **Be aware of sensory issues**: The most important step in coping is becoming more aware of your own sensory issues and how it affects you. Having a sensory assessment by a specially trained occupational therapist might be helpful.

(c) **Be your own advocate and learn to take care of yourself:** Be assertive and be your own advocate. Give yourself permission to be who you are with your sensory sensitivities.

(d) **Explain to others such as friends and family about sensory sensitivities:** Tell people what the issues are and why you avoid certain situations or foods. Seek their understanding.

(e) **Avoidance of the stimuli and modification of the environment is often the best**: Although avoidance is generally not a good strategy to adopt in life, it may be necessary to give yourself permission to avoid certain overstimulating unpleasant situations. Be assertive and modify your environment when needed. For example, ask for a quiet table in a restaurant, or ask for the music to be turned down.

(f) **Carry a portable sensory first aid kit:** It may also help to carry a portable sensory repair kit with you including items such as a pair of sunglasses, ear plugs to block out bright light or loud noises, a pleasant scent that is relaxing, a book or computer game to distract yourself.

(g) **Systematic desensitisation:** If somebody has a phobia and exposes themselves to the phobic object, such as a spider, there is normally a process called habituation, where their anxiety generally and gradually goes down. This does not appear to happen so readily with AS-type sensory sensitivities as there appears to be no habituation. However, a degree of desensitisation can increase your tolerance or threshold for coping and make life more bearable.

(h) **Self-talk can help:** With maturity, you can develop a greater ability to endure sensory experiences by using strategies such as self-talk. Saying, for example, 'This won't last long; I'll be out of here in 10 minutes' or 'Be brave, I can cope with this' may help to override the impulse to escape quickly and extend tolerance levels.

(i) **Be practical, control and diminish discomfort:** Be practical and control the things that you can control, so that you are not too stressed, so that when the unexpected occurs, you have a better chance of coping. For example, wear clothes that are comfortable.

(j) **Make your home a sensory-safe comfort base**: If you are going to face sensory challenges in the outside world, make sure you have some safe and comfortable place to retreat back to.

10 Synaesthesia and creative thought

Synaesthesia is a complex sensory phenomenon where there is a blending of sensation, perception and emotion. The most common type is where a person might see numbers as colours; for example, number three is seen as blue. But other people report tasting a colour, seeing a sound, hearing a shape, seeing faces with coloured halos, or emotions provoking a certain colour. The condition is thought to be because of an anomaly in the wiring of the brain, where there is cross wiring or cross activation. It is no coincidence that the main colour area of the brain is the fusiform gyrus of the temporal lobe, which is the same general area that specialises in numbers and faces. It could be that the wiring for number has mistakenly been put in the neighbouring socket for colour, so that the person sees colour for numbers.

Ramachandra (2013) points out that many artists and poets – Kandinsky, Pollock, Nabakov, Liszt – had or have synaesthesia, and he estimates that one-sixth of all creative people have the condition. His research also suggests that synaeasethia has a genetic component and runs in families. It is often the ability to forge links between seemingly unrelated domains of the brain, linking unrelated words, images and ideas, that is the core of creativity. A poet or writer who creates a metaphor is in a sense creating a link between two domains, linking seemingly unrelated concepts, words, images and ideas. Our ability to uncover hidden analogies is the basis of creative thought. Shakespeare was particularly good at creating metaphors and imagery. One of my favourites is, 'Friends, grapple them to the soul, with hoops of steel'. There must have been a good connection, a bundle of long white fibres, between Shakespeare's vocabulary or word part of his brain and the visual–spatial pictorial areas.

11 Motor coordination and clumsiness problems

It is estimated that 80 per cent of people with AS have problems with motor coordination or clumsiness. The first indicators are often difficulties learning to walk, which might be delayed by a few months. When older, children might also show difficulties learning to dress, tie up shoelaces, use a knife, fork, scissors, do up buttons, knot a neck tie or learn to skate. They may also show clumsiness or have a tendency to bump into things. They may have an odd gait when running or walking and an ungainly lack of coordination and synchronicity between upper and lower limbs. Others might have difficulty catching or throwing a ball, which is to do with timing and poor coordination. Some children walk without the associated arm swing or have a problem with balance and therefore find riding a bicycle very difficult; others might have a problem clapping in rhythm. And for some, handwriting might be an indecipherable scrawl.

People with AS are often not very good at team sports that require fine coordination although some have become good at solitary sport such as long-distance running, where a low tolerance for discomfort is an advantage, or individual sports such as golf, swimming, rock climbing, archery, horse riding or martial arts. Sometimes people with AS receive a separate diagnosis of dyspraxia, a condition specifically associated with motor coordination problems and difficulty conceptualising or planning movement. Others might have involuntary tic, which might be motor or verbal or facial twitches as in Tourette's syndrome. As stated in chapter 2, the part of the brain called the cerebellum – concerned with the calibration, integration and coordination of fine motor movement, dexterity, timing and sensory systems – is smaller in people with AS, which may explain the following problems:

- 'I never had a sense of natural grace; it was as if my brain and body were not connected properly. When I played football at school my feet would get all tangled up and I'd often miss the ball.'
- 'The pencil did not obey me; it just felt awkward in my hand.'
- 'I always felt disconnected between my body and my brain and really struggle to keep in time with a rhythm if people are clapping to music.'
- 'I walk into things. Sometimes I walk down the stairs and forget how to walk.'
- 'Sometimes my shadow is my best friend because it shows me what I'm doing. I don't have a sense of my body in space.'

Chapter Eight

Emotions

1 Understanding and processing our emotions

How many men have been accused of being insensitive in emotional situations? How many women have been accused of being oversensitive? Do we experience emotions too intensely or not intensely enough? Do we get the balance right between thinking and feeling – mind and heart? The issues that people with AS struggle with can be a mirror to help us all understand ourselves more fully. One man with AS said to me once: 'How can I understand the emotions in another person if I can't understand the emotions in myself?'

Research studies have shown that from an early age, autistic children are not predisposed or wired up to want to interact with those closest to them. This often presents as difficulties with making eye contact, recognising and understanding facial expressions in others. There is an area of the brain called the fusiform gyrus, or face area, part of the temporal and occipital lobe, which is specifically concerned with deciphering faces. Research has shown that there are consistently lower levels of activation in this area in people with AS compared to neurotypical controls. This suggests the person with AS lacks the vital equipment to fully understand the social and emotional world which is full of facial expressions, subtle complex nuances, gestures, intonations and figures of speech, hidden meanings and fleeting glances expressing a range of potentially confusing and illogical emotions.

Our understanding and experience of our own feelings is due to a combination of the wiring of our brain and the environment that we were brought up in. The first ingredient is an ideal brain that is fully connected, with thick bands of neural pathways from sensory and emotional areas in the heart of the brain, such as the amygdala, to the frontal lobe areas of the brain. These neural pathways also connect the right side to the left side of the brain, across the connecting bridge known as the corpus collosum. There would be a smooth transmission, backwards and forwards, between thought and feelings. However, this is not always the case in the brain of an individual with AS. One suggestion is that the insula, a key relay station on the pathway between our sensory brain and frontal lobes, is less active in those with AS. The insula is folded within the fissure between the frontal and temporal lobes and its job is to receive signals from all the visceral organs in the body, such as the heart, lungs, liver, bones, muscles and skin. It then forms a map of the sensations that are being experienced in the different parts of the body. The insula then passes on the information, for example, 'My heart is beating quickly; I must be anxious or excited'. It might be that some people with AS don't get those messages so clearly and therefore lack awareness of bodily feelings and sensations that reflect emotions. The technical term is a lack of 'interoception', which means the person can be, in effect, blind or deaf to their own bodily sensations or states, including emotions. Often people with AS need to deliberately monitor and scan their body, checking it out with an emotional thermometer, to get a clue as to how they are feeling.

The second ingredient for a flourishing emotional system is an environment where the initial caregivers are tuned in and synchronised to the emotions and behaviours of the baby. There is an emotional attachment, love that bonds baby and carer, so they respond in a sensitive synchronised sequence, reinforcing, mirroring expressions and gestures, explaining and labelling emotions. The babies, then toddlers, learn how to react to their environment, and their emotional repertoire develops from a few basic impulses, such as crying and smiling, to more complex sophisticated emotions. However, if babies have AS and are not programmed or tuned in to the neurotypical world, or the parent with neurotypicality is not tuned in to the autistic world, this synchronised responding is more difficult to achieve.

2 Differences in the way people with Asperger's syndrome process emotions

Inevitably, for the person with AS, the world of emotions is not as easily understood as the logical, rational world associated with numbers, rules, structures and systems. There are structures around emotions, but they are rather indistinct and vague and the person with AS is less in tune with them. In conversation with people with AS, patterns of different emotional responses seem to emerge with certain features.

(a) Time delay

There is evidence of a slower speed of information processing and reduced efficiency in switching attentional channels in people with AS. Temple Grandin uses the metaphor of people with AS having a 'dial-up' rather than 'high-speed internet connection'. This may result in people with AS reporting that they are slower to process emotion as indicated in the following quotations:

- 'It takes a while for the emotion to percolate through. It's like my timing is different and I'm on a time delay. I cope with the facts first, then the emotions take over so I'm not overloaded. I don't process things as smoothly. Sometimes I store things up and then explode or have a meltdown – it's all or nothing.'
- 'I've always had a strong emotional disconnect. I get it on a cognitive level but not on a feeling level. There might be a three-day delay.'
- 'My strongest emotional reactions are often delayed and it took me almost a month to cry after my grandmother's funeral.'
- 'I cannot show emotion and intellect at the same time.'

(b) Different degrees of emotion

A further, frequently reported comment is that people with AS experience greater extremes of emotion. Many are hypoemotional, experiencing a general lower level of emotions. Others are hyperemotional, experiencing peaks and spikes, just like with other senses. Temple Grandin explains: 'My emotions are all in the present. I can be angry but I get over it quickly. When I replay a scene the emotions are no longer attached to them.' Grandin goes on to say that 'I am what I do, not what I feel' and says she doesn't get complex lingering emotions. A person with AS might approach emotions in a logical way with more thinking than feeling. Other people have made the following comments:

- 'There are advantages to being unemotional. My girlfriend said she liked me because I was always calm, steady and "like a rock", in a crisis. I'm very logical and just think things through. I think I'd be a very good doctor in A&E.'
- 'At my grandmother's funeral I pretended I was sad like everybody else and had to restrain myself from being silly and trying to cheer everybody up.'
- 'I'm "aemotional", if that is a word – I'm not happy or sad. I'm just here. Sometimes I do have emotional responses; sometimes I don't; sometimes I don't know. Most of the time I'm just OK.'
- 'If I go into a shop I never choose anything spontaneously. I never have that "gut reaction". All my decisions are based on too much logical appraisal.'

(c) All or nothing emotions – switching on and off

Closely linked to not feeling certain emotions is the notion that for many people with AS, their feelings are either black (bad, negative) or white (good, happy neutral) – 'all or nothing' – with no shades of grey, nothing in the middle. Jenny wrote the following description of her experience of emotion:

> My mind doesn't realise it's feeling something until the very last minute; then it's very extreme. Now I'm beginning to recognise more when I'm feeling emotion – particularly since I got my diagnosis and am seeing a

> therapist. I notice my breathing is becoming quicker and I get a bit shaky if I'm becoming anxious, or if there are tears behind my eyes I'm feeling sad, or that the sandbag on top of my heart is lifted when I feel relaxed. I now make a list, a sort of diary and connect things up in my mind. I don't pick up internal bodily messages very well so I can't tell if I'm hungry, or if my bladder is full, until the very last minute. It's the same with feeling stressed – It's rather black and white like a switch – all or nothing!

(d) Somatisation – emotion expressed physically

When we are stressed, there are often physical manifestations of that stress – we might be more prone to a cold, headache or diarrhoea – but often people with AS lack that awareness of the emotion of stress and just see the physical manifestation. For some the physical manifestation might 'come out of the blue'. Tony's comments highlight this tendency:

> Before I got my diagnosis if somebody had said to me, 'Do you have anxiety', I'd have said, 'No'. But I did have this thing called 'unexplained nausea', where I would vomit and then feel physically drained. I've since realised that was my anxiety – that was how my body expressed it; I just wasn't good at sensing it.

(e) Discomfort with strong emotion in others

Many people with AS are uncomfortable with prolonged high emotional intensity in others, possibly due to not having those feelings themselves and not being equipped to interpret and respond.

- 'Emotions of others make me feel uncomfortable. They seem exaggerated, gushing and overly demonstrative.'
- 'Expressing emotions is difficult. Females are often all huggy and kissy, which is not my cup of tea. I can feel something quite profound inside, but it doesn't always show on my face.'
- 'My first boyfriend was all over me like a rash. He'd always want to touch, hold hands and tell me he loved me – it drove me mad. He had to go. My husband is much cooler and unemotional and it suits me better.'

(f) Alexithymia – lack of words for emotions

Alexithymia is a term coined to describe a state of deficiency in understanding, processing or describing emotions. Alexithymia literally means, 'without words for mood or emotions'. It is inversely related to concepts such as 'psychological mindedness', 'emotional intelligence' and 'introspection'. It involves difficulty identifying feelings and distinguishing between feelings and bodily sensations and difficulty describing feelings to other people. Alexithymia is thought to be greater in males than females and occurs in less than 10 per cent of the general population (although over 50 per cent of the autistic population). The answer to the question 'How are you feeling?' is often very difficult because the person doesn't know and doesn't have the words to provide an answer. The research literature has distinguished primary and secondary alexithymia: primary being a condition people are born with, due to the neurological wiring of the brain; and secondary, due to a trauma or series of trauma which produces a psychological reaction.

- 'I find it hard to explain how I feel. I know I cannot describe my emotions. I can't put words to them.'
- 'Sometimes I feel my emotions in colours rather than words.'

3 Understanding and recognising emotion in others

This skill involves being able to read the emotional expression of another person mainly through interpreting facial expression, voice intonation and non-verbal body language. This is largely a cognitive skill but also involves having a shared referent of understanding, being able to identify those same emotions in themselves.

- 'Animals I understand, people I don't. At least animals are honest. If an animal doesn't like you, it growls. If a person doesn't like you, they might smile.'
- 'Nico can work out what's going on emotionally, but it's not intuitive or natural; he works it out like a mathematical puzzle; it's all logic.'

- 'If you don't signpost emotions, I just don't pick them up. I don't do non-verbals. There is no point hinting you might as well just say it.'
- 'Because things don't have an emotional impact on me, I assume they don't have an impact on others. I assume that people just want the facts but I'm beginning to realise that this is not always right. If I have a disagreement with my wife I try to emphasise the facts and the mistakes the facts were causing – a simple fact check could spare wounded feelings and everybody would be happier. She said my search for accuracy and quest for facts was not helpful and was irritating and I needed to focus on her hurt. She said, "Hurt feelings don't respond to your facts".'

4 Empathy

Empathy is our ability to identify what someone else is thinking and feeling and to respond to their thoughts and feelings with an appropriate emotion. It can be divided into three components: cognitive empathy (knowing); emotional empathy (feeling); and compassionate empathy (responding).

Cognitive empathy (knowing) is the capacity to comprehend or read another person's point of view and is largely identified with an area of the frontal lobes called the orbitofrontal cortex. It involves the ability to read body language, facial expressions, tone of voice and other non-verbal behaviour, in order to understand the degree of distress of another person. If the emotional signals are obvious, such as the person is crying, it is possible to read that emotion. It is rather like reading the headlines in a newspaper. But if the emotion is subtle, it is more difficult to read, like reading the small print of the article. For most people with AS the cognitive aspects of empathy are impaired.

Emotional or affective empathy (feeling) is the ability to vicariously experience the emotion of another person, 'I feel what you feel'.

A phenomenon sometimes termed 'emotional contagion' or 'emotional mirroring' is associated with an area of the brain, the superior temporal cortex and prefrontal cortex. It is the ability to feel someone else's distress and to resonate with and absorb someone else's feelings – to be able to 'put yourself in someone else's shoes'. If a person with AS has never experienced those emotions they have nothing to remember back to, no personal experience of that emotional depth, and therefore they may have difficulty achieving empathy. However, many people with AS have good affective or emotional empathy once they have identified the other person's distress, although some do not.

Compassionate empathy (responding) is the ability to know how to respond to somebody feeling distressed in a sympathetic and appropriate manner. A prerequisite is that the person has first read the signals that the person is distressed. There is often a fear of making a mistake or rejection when deciding how to respond and with what intensity. Persons with AS have their own reaction to distress which might be to be left alone and therefore they're not very good at providing the conventional words and gestures of compassion and affection for other people.

Empathy requires a double-minded focus of attention, to be able to attend to both ourselves and the other person. Empathy is reduced the more we become single-minded or self-focused, losing sight of the other person. It means being aware of how we come across to others and acknowledging others' feelings and actions. The advantages of having good empathy include (1) being able to find solutions to social conflicts or relationship problems; (2) being able to avoid the risk of misunderstanding or miscommunication by figuring out what the other person intended; (3) avoiding causing offence by anticipating how things will be experienced by the other person; (4) making the other person feel valued and acknowledged increasing the quality of intimate relationships and close long-term friendships. Without empathy, a person is often left isolated in their own little bubble.

The following comments give a flavour of what people with AS say about empathy:

- 'If someone's upset I prefer practical help such as making them a cup of tea, getting tissues or giving solutions – I'm not really a hugger.'
- 'Empathy doesn't come naturally for someone who lacks the ability to take another person's perspective.'
- 'I'm a nurse on ITU and I've learned to say to parents, "I'm really sorry your baby died". But actually I don't feel really sorry.'
- 'I've learnt to say, "I'm sorry I don't know what you are feeling but I do care".'
- 'One of my colleagues whom I manage had a sudden death in the family and was very upset. I did what I had seen people do in films and touched her on the shoulder and said, "You go home; don't worry about anything here at work". I think I managed the situation quite well but it was a bit like I was acting in a film.'
- 'If there are three steps involved in empathy, I miss out on them all. I don't intuitively notice; I don't really feel or care; and I don't act.'

Many people with AS do experience high levels of empathy and many work in the caring professions. For some, it may not be intuitive and they may need support to notice the signs of distress in others and intellectually make those links and connections.

5 Love and jealousy

Generally most people with AS are more prone to brief low-intensity expression of affection, having a limited tolerance of sentimentality in others, and can feel overwhelmed with greater levels of expressive affection. However, at the other extreme, people with AS can have very intense obsessive emotional reactions.

One young man called Andrew commented: 'I find it difficult to say, "I love you" to my family. When I was a child and I had to write a birthday or Christmas cards for my family I never put kisses or signed it "Love Andrew" – that would have felt wrong.' A similar honest comment was made by Rachel, a woman in her mid-thirties:

> 'I will never understand love; it doesn't make sense to me. I understand fear and anger; they are tangible real emotions, but love is just too abstract. I understand that I can physically fancy somebody, I know when I enjoy talking to them, or when I like them, but how do you know when you love somebody?'.

Both Andrew and Rachel have very logical, precise minds which perhaps do not allow them to use the word love carelessly. Perhaps the word love is overused today in broader society? Many people with AS wonder why neurotypicals are so obsessed with being told they are loved. The word love as a concept is huge and covers a multitude of different feelings and has many implications. Is it the rather precise pedantic use of language or is it the lack of actual feelings that holds Andrew and Rachel back from using the word love – or a combination of both? The ancient Greeks had at least four different words for love: *agape* – unconditional love of god and family; *eros* – erotic, sensuous love; *philia* – friendship, affection and *storge* – an empathic bond or fondness. Perhaps Andrew would be more comfortable if the definition of love was more precise and specified and he could have said, 'I feel agape love for you, Mum?'

At the other extreme, Jade was prone to developing whirlwind attachments and infatuations, with such intensity and focus, that everything else in life was swept away. She commented:

> It was awful, I was completely obsessed with him and kept contacting him. It was so all consuming. There was no moderation. I felt like the mythical Greek character Icarus, flying into the sun. I knew my wings would burn and I'd come crashing to the ground, but I just couldn't stop myself. I drove him away and was devastated.

Neuroscience experiments scanned the brains of people in love, when they were shown pictures of their loved ones. They demonstrated two reactions. There was a heightened activation in the social engagement and reward system of the brain (anterior cingulate, insula, caudate nucleus and putamen) and a decrease in activity of the areas of the brain normally associated with threat (amygdala, posterior cingulate and areas of the right side). The threat system scanning the environment for external fear is deactivated or stood down at a neural level. Love seems to be a combination of at least two processes – a reduction in fear or threat and an increase in the social engagement and reward system – combined with an activation of biochemical networks throughout our brains. Perhaps if a person with AS has less active social engagement and reward system and a more active threat system, it is more difficult to experience love?

People with AS might not be traditional loving demonstrative partners, wanting to hold hands and cuddle, but they can be caring and affectionate engendering a feeling of love in others. Partners of people with AS and workers have made the following comments:

- 'My husband is not affectionate, but he does do a lot for me – he earns the money, looks after the house – and I know his deeds show that he does love me but he has difficulty showing it.'
- 'I love Jane because she's different, loyal, and above all honest. But, at times I do feel lonely and empty, because I know she can't tap into my needs.'
- 'My husband rarely tells me he loves me. He told me once: "Look nothing has changed; I told you when we got married that I love you". I said, "Yes, but that was five years ago!"'.
- 'I was a teacher support worker for a young man with AS at university for two years and saw him most days. On my final day I really wanted him to ask me about myself or say "how are you today?" but he didn't. I felt disappointed.'

The experience of jealousy is a complex emotion that can also illustrate something about the emotions of people with AS. I saw a couple once; the husband with AS had upset his neurotypical wife by being 'overfriendly', and slightly inappropriate with another woman at a barbeque. The wife felt jealous, saying to her husband, 'Didn't you see how she was coming on to you and how you were encouraging her, laughing and joking and standing too close'. The husband did not interpret the event in the same way and could not understand the emotion of jealousy; he said: 'why on earth would you feel like that?; it doesn't make sense', which the wife felt as very dismissive. The husband was not at all emotional, and prided himself on never feeling worry, doubt or negative emotions such as jealousy and was rather intolerant of his wife's emotions calling them irrational and childish. The wife was more emotional and worried experiencing jealousy. The husband went on to say:

> I don't feel jealous, never have and don't understand it. To me it is completely irrational. I told my wife that I love her, we have a son, so what more does she want to know? She asked me how I would feel if we were to separate and I said I would be very sad but that it would not be the end of the world. If she wanted to go off with somebody else I wouldn't stop her – I don't want to control her. I would try to detach myself, unhook myself and try to put the loss aside. She said she felt devastated that I felt so little and that I was so dismissive. How she is feeling just doesn't make sense to me.

Just to prove how diverse the AS population is, Katherine, a lady in her mid-thirties, recently diagnosed with AS, described her experience of jealousy. 'I know what jealousy is as I've always been jealous of my younger brother. From the day he was born I didn't want him as he took my parent's attention away from me. I never referred to him by his real name, but always calling him "boy" and either deliberately ignored him or was unpleasant to him.'

6 Ways of improving emotional attunement

Emotional attunement training: Children diagnosed early with AS sometimes get the opportunity to engage in 'affective or emotional education', where they can learn about the world of emotions, just as one might learn a foreign language. These special training programmes are devoted to learning how to read emotions in themselves and others. Other programmes include using comic strip stories, where the AS person is supported to identify others' intentions, how others may feel and what they may be thinking by filling in speech and thought bubbles.

Psychotherapy/cognitive behavioural therapy (CBT): Psychological therapy is about helping people make links and connections between situations, feelings and thoughts and to self-reflect. It is advantageous if the therapist knows about AS and is directive, pragmatic, focusing on working out practical solutions and offering structured sessions. The type of 'meaningful silences' found in non-directive psychoanalytical therapy is definitely best avoided. It is often helpful to have third party involved in a session rather than always purely 1 to 1 as this provides external support and prompting and a link to autobiographical memory.

Learning through imitation: Many people with AS say they deliberately read or watch TV to learn about empathic responses.

- 'I've watched hundreds of hours of TV humorous sitcoms, like "Friends" about people having relationships and humorous conversations about random things. I even tried memorising the dialogue.'
- 'Reading fiction has helped me to understand how people think and feel.'
- 'I've learned how to do attentive listening and make empathic comments such as "oh dear", or "how sad for you" or "Mmm" or just nodding.'

Using different mediums to express emotions: You don't always have to speak your emotions. Many people with AS find it easier to explain how they feel by using text messages or email.

- 'I find typing a message online much easier than talking to somebody face to face.'
- 'I dance to express my emotions – I find it a great release.'
- 'I have become better at verbalising my emotions but sometimes my facial expression doesn't match up.
- 'I can't find words for my emotions but I can draw a picture. My feelings are like a jagged graph or the teeth of a saw''

7 Understanding and coping with 'meltdowns'

Not all people with AS have meltdowns, but many do. A meltdown by definition is an extreme, involuntary, emotional and behavioural response to a stressful situation that is usually caused by sensory, cognitive or social triggers. There are usually few warning signs. One moment the individual could be content and the next completely out of control. Although the diagnosed persons themselves might not notice warning signs, an outsider might notice subtle signs such as more pressured speech, being slightly less coherent or an increase in repetitive behaviours. The persons' reactions are invariably a 'fight', 'flight' or 'freeze' and might be an explosion of frustration or anger, running away for self-preservation, tears, self-injurious behaviour – such as biting themselves on their forearm or banging their head, or a retreat into themselves such as sitting in the corner humming or carrying out some other repetitive behaviour. Sometimes it might be a small trivial event which is the last straw to tip the balance. The explosiveness of a meltdown seems to be because adrenaline, a stress hormone, is released too quickly. Afterwards the person may feel physically and mentally exhausted and also feel guilty, ashamed and remorseful. A large emotional reaction or meltdown, where feelings are vented briefly, helps clear the system – it is a failsafe, a release of all that pent-up adrenaline. The AS person feels physically better afterwards and recovers quickly, but might feel intense feelings of remorse, embarrassment or shame. However, others involved might continue to feel devastated with hurt feelings.

Rita reported that she had a meltdown at a music festival:

> I had been to another music festival, which was just about OK. I planned meticulously and thought that I'd taken every precaution, making lists and back up plans but it all went wrong. I think it was a combination of a lack of sleep, too many people, too many strangers who were friends of friends and it was just too social, too chaotic, out of control. I just flipped and was shaking, trembling, crying, couldn't make sense, literally collapsed. People were trying to be helpful getting me to walk. I just needed to be in a quiet dark comfortable place. I left the festival and felt better and just wanted to sleep.

It is important to recognise the potential triggers to a meltdown.

- Novel situations or sudden abrupt changes or unplanned events.
- Sensory overload: loud noise, chaos, bright florescent lights, crowds, strong smells, people's touch.
- Transitions from school to work or moving house or changing jobs.
- Being time pressured, pushed or hurried.
- Conversations, including sub-conversations or multiple people talking.
- Communication where people are vague, non-specific or imprecise saying things such as, 'How do you feel?', or 'Just a minute', vague instructions or open-ended questions.
- Social contact that goes on, where there isn't a time limit and no escape.

When confronting someone in meltdown avoid the following as it may inflame the situation:

- Don't raise your voice.
- Don't ask them what's wrong – they won't know or they may not be able to articulate this.
- Don't ask questions or offer choices.
- Don't use sarcasm.
- Don't use physical restraint.

Instead

- Use a quiet but assertive voice and focus on distraction or a more constructive way of releasing the energy.
- Encourage them to have some time out or solitude to calm down.
- Encourage engagement with some physical activity, to burn it off or engage in their own strategy such as self-stimming.
- It may help 'just to be a presence' and say nothing or offer a short reassuring phrase, such as, 'It's going to be OK'.

Tips for coping with meltdowns

- Try to identify the stressors and triggers for meltdowns. Sensory, cognitive and social? Can any of them be prevented or reduced?
- Devise your own 'stress thermometer' and rate your level of stress from 0 to 100.
- Try to become aware of overload and regulate and plan your life so that you are not overwhelmed. Think ahead, have a plan and prepare.
- Have a stress level repair kit, which might be listening to your favourite music on headphones or inhaling a favourite smell or playing a game on your phone.
- Have a proper diet, exercise and burn off that adrenaline, get enough sleep and commune with nature.
- Engage in physical movement, exercise, to vent and release that rising adrenaline – flap your hands if necessary.

- Try to correct the underlying cause of the meltdown, by reducing the stimulation levels.
- Breathe deeply and count to 10, which is simple but sometimes effective.
- Have an escape strategy – go somewhere to be alone or something to do to de- stress.
- Talk to somebody, emotionally unburden yourself and allow the listener to piece it all together. Seek advice – it helps to share a problem.
- Apologise, show signs of remorse; you might feel better but the others are likely to still feel upset.

Chapter Nine

Relationships and social life

1 The need for social life and friendship

For people with AS, socialising does not come naturally, but is often an effort and can be tiring. Hans Asperger (1944, p58) said:

> 'Normal children acquire the necessary social habits without being consciously aware of them, they learn instinctively. It is these instinctive social relations that are disturbed in autistic children. Social adaptation has to proceed via the intellect.'

There is a clash of culture between the autistic and neurotypical world over socialising. Those with AS might perceive some people in the neurotypical world as social zealots, prioritising socialising above anything else and expecting everybody to find socialising easy, natural and rewarding. They might discriminate against those that don't, seeing them as defective or weird.

A compromise is needed between the two cultures. There is a paradox in that socialising and friendship can be one of the biggest insulators against stress, low mood, low self-esteem, and can also act in the role of protector from real or perceived threats and help with problem solving. But at the same time friendships can be one of the biggest causes of stress and depression.

2 Capacity for socialising – 'I fill up quickly'

We all have different capacities for socialising; some people are naturally intuitively comfortable in a social situation, whereas for others it requires effort and energy. As a rule people with AS feel more comfortable if social interactions are brief, purposeful and have a fixed ending as they need to go away and recharge their batteries. Liane Holliday Willey (2007, p43) commented about her level or desire for socialisation, 'To me friends were people I enjoyed a few minutes or a few hours with ... I fill up quickly'. James commented:

> I actually like some social situations as long as they are time limited and preferably structured. So meeting for a purpose to play a game is better than just meeting to 'chill out' or be at a party. But after a while I'm used up, spent, I've said what I want to say and need a break, some restoration time, time on my own. I can do socialising but two hours is my maximum. It helps to know when it's going to be over.

Solitude is a natural state for people with AS and is also the most effective emotional restorative, a way of calming down. It is understandable why many young men with AS retreat to the sanctuary and refuge of their bedroom, with online computer games.

3 Two's company; three's a crowd

People with AS can function reasonably well sometimes in a one-to-one social situation but when things get more complicated and there are three or four people, difficulties become more apparent – two's company three's a crowd. These difficulties often involve the person with AS having slower information processing and not being able to process all the necessary social cues fast enough to stay synchronised with the conversation of the group. They might get left behind. One person reported that in a group situation she would often find herself not being able to keep up and having to refer back saying, 'Going back to what you were just saying, I think ...'

Socialising involves numerous skills, particularly the art of 'small talk'. Imagine a situation of a group of people waiting to start a course, or milling around at a party. What are the skills involved in starting a conversation? First, reading the other person's face and body language to see whether they are friendly, approachable and want to engage in conversation: what mood are they in, what is their intention? Starting a conversation involves stringing a few sentences together – an opener – which could be a question or at least something appropriate. The words need to be matched with a friendly demeanour, appropriate facial expressions, gestures and tone of voice. Then there is responding to the other person's talk, keeping the conversation going, straying into and sharing mutual areas of interest. This involves recognising that the other person might not want to talk about a particular special interest and picking up the cues that they might be bored. Then there is the business of subtly and lightly disengaging and moving off and talking to somebody else.

The subtle art of socialising involves that key skill of being able to do two things at the same time. To simultaneously be able to listen to the other person, respond non-verbally with eye contact, nods and grunts, and at the same time formulate your own feelings and responses and then deliver that response appropriately in synch with the other person. People with AS by definition find it difficult to take another person's perspective, do two things at the same time and identify their own thoughts and feelings. The term 'reciprocal social interaction' means taking turns in a synchronised backwards and forwards conversation, where one person doesn't dominate too much – like a game of table tennis the conversation bounces backwards and forwards.

It is important for people with AS to know the rules and reasons behind social behaviour – to understand the logic. I remember an AS lady called Theresa who was in the territorial army and used to go away at weekends, which I assumed would involve a lot of stressful socialising. She enlightened me by saying, 'Socialising in the army officers' mess is much easier than anywhere I've ever come across as there are specific rules about who you speak to and how you speak'.

4 Friendship

Friendships and relationships are complicated, emotional and unpredictable, which is all very challenging for people with AS, who often report as having fewer friendships and present as struggling to maintain relationships with less satisfying social lives.

People with AS have certain qualities that make them good friends and partners. They can be undeniably loyal, trustworthy, dependable, honest and truthful, straightforward, confident about their opinions, relatively independent, happy to amuse themselves, usually calm, rational, dependable in a crisis and happy to share practical knowledge. They can be compassionate towards others as they may have been the victim of teasing and bullying themselves. People with AS don't need to gossip or pry into the affairs of others and are often committed to the best interest of others. People with AS will often 'go the extra mile' for a friend, not knowing the word 'quit' and try to hang on to friendships, finding it particularly hurtful when others might break a friendship. People with AS often expect too much from friends and can have standards that are impossible to reach. If somebody says they will 'call', the AS individual will expect this to happen and if it doesn't will get extremely upset.

Tips for making friends for those with Asperger's syndrome

- It is important to get out and meet people. Join a special interest group, or a group where there is a common subject to talk about, like cycling.
- Use the internet to link up with people who might have a similar special interest.
- Approach people who have room for and value an extra friend, not somebody who is already too busy and popular.
- Try to develop the right degree of intensity by building friendships gradually, not too intensely; otherwise the other person might be scared off. Similarly, try not to be too shy; otherwise the other person might think the person is not interested.
- Learn how to recognise predators, danger from strangers and manipulation. Check out the suitability of the friendship with someone else. Is the friendship balanced? Does the person have honest/positive intentions?

5 School, bullying and finding a mentor

School is often a stressful and mentally exhausting environment where people with AS work twice as hard as other children because they not only have to cope with the academic demands but the social demands as well. They are people who need a break more than most. Schools can be inhabited by predators and bullies. Children with AS need solitude to recharge their batteries and are often found in a quiet room, the library or the chess club.

Research suggests that children with AS are bullied four times more than neurotypical children and that 90 per cent of mothers of AS children reported that their children had been bullied. Stories of being the last person picked for sports teams or wandering around the playground on their own are common. Children with AS are vulnerable to bullying because often they are shy, passive, do not have many friends to protect them, are academically very competent, poor at sports, and wear clothes for comfort rather than for fashion. They are also socially naive and eager to be part of a group and have poor social antennae for identifying the predators and distinguishing between the kind and unkind peers. One man said:

> 'I was bullied at school, but the main problem was that I couldn't see it coming. People would ask me questions, some to wind me up maliciously, but others might genuinely want to know. I couldn't discern which was genuine and which was a wind-up – I couldn't pick the good guys from the bad guys.'

Teenage girls with AS are particularly vulnerable to sexual exploitation due to their naiveté, or lack of social antennae, where they don't recognise that the intentions of others might be sexual or malevolent. It helps to have a mentor and Liane Holliday Willey (1999, p40) touchingly describes a boy called Craig who throughout her school career offered mentorship and protection, 'Craig jumped in to rescue me even before I knew I needed to be rescued'. Everybody with AS in the school situation would benefit from a Craig.

6 Ways of coping with the social world

- Drama is a useful activity for helping people to learn social skills, particularly as they can't rely on their instinct and intuition. It teaches body language, facial expression, tone of voice, responses for situations, and creates and models understanding of complex social situations. A mother of an 18-year-old AS girl said, 'Having Katherine join a drama group at the age of 12 was the best decision we ever made as she learned so much about social skills and how to act in social situations'.
- People can learn social skills by watching television or films, modelling or imitating their peers or by getting specialist help.
- Martial arts, such as Taekwondo, are often popular coping strategies for people with AS because they increase skills in self-protection, act as a deterrent against bullying and also help teach skills about remaining calm. It is also a rather solitary sport, which requires a great deal of structured repetition and practice, often ideal for somebody with autistic traits.
- Working with animals is a good way to meet like-minded companions as people with AS frequently have an uncanny ability to relate to and communicate with animals.

7 Marriage and romantic partnerships

In many ways, people with AS have qualities that make them a suitable partner. They are likely to have a different way of thinking, tending to be logical, pragmatic and straightforward rather than emotional. If there is a problem the AS approach is more likely to be practical, 'Let's try to find a practical way to fix it and make each other happy', rather than having moodiness, hidden subterranean feelings, drama, sulking, volatility and lingering resentments. They are also likely to be honest, loyal and happy to be alone, quite capable of occupying their own time with their special interest, rather than being 'clingy or dependant'.

However, there are obvious problems that make a romantic relationship difficult as the AS partner might prefer more solitude and time alone rather than socialising, may have special interests that give them satisfaction, rather than the quality of the interpersonal relationship itself, may prefer structure rather than spontaneity and may not pick up on the emotional needs of their partner. The most common complaint of a neurotypical partner married to a person with AS is that they feel lonely and miss out on regular affectionate affirmations, gestures or loving words. The person with AS is generally not consistently emotionally demonstrative.

Relationships between somebody with AS and a neurotypical are often complex, where there might be an attraction of opposites – both give something different which makes a whole – in simplistic terms, one does most of the thinking and one might do more of the feeling. The neurotypical partner might also have a role as the 'executive secretary', helping with organisational problems and planning, and also act as the social secretary. It is noticeable that many people with AS have sympathetic understanding, partners – often people who work in the caring professions, such as nurses, counsellors or social workers – who offer a degree of emotional support, mentoring and guidance in the social world. Sometimes that person offers some of the features of a mother figure.

Most people with AS have a desire and need for an intimate relationship, and it is only a small percentage that would not fall into that category. People with AS certainly have strong feelings and a great capacity to love, but the difficulties come with the lack of social skills to build a relationship and the ability to read other people's emotions and in sustaining the relationship.

Techniques to improve AS relationship or marriage:

The Asperger Couple's Workbook, by Maxine Aston (2009), gives practical advice and useful strategies to help couples in a relationship, where one partner has Asperger's. She makes the point that communication is a major problem as both partners are on a different wavelength and speak a different language. One is logical, linear, one subject at a time and the other is likely to be more emotional and unpredictable. Some useful tips include the following:

- *No distractions.* If having an important conversation, make sure the TV and radio are off, there are no other people present, you are not eating or driving and you have time.
- *The colour communication system.* This is a visual form of communicating rather than using words, as words can be hurtful, or difficult, particularly in the heat of an argument. The couple can use actual coloured cards, like a set of traffic lights or the referee's card used in football. A red card stands for danger, meaning, 'We need to stop; pause this debate as I'm frightened it will get out of control'. A yellow card stands for uncertainty, meaning, 'I don't fully understand what you mean; please can we go back and you tell me in a way I can understand'. A green card means, 'I'm OK with what you have told me. I understand'. Another option is a bracelet, which has two sides which can be flipped: a red side which means, 'Leave me alone' and green is 'I'm OK'. On other occasions emotions can be expressed in colours and perhaps numbered. So 'red 9' means, 'I need time on my own urgently'.
- *The anger thermometer.* Visualise a thermometer with a 10-point scale and when anger or frustration increases, the red liquid rises

up the scale towards 10. If a couple are having a disagreement and one partner is feeling frustrated they could simply interject, 'My thermometer is at 8', which informs the other that it's time to pause and diffuse the tension.

- *Check out assumptions*. It is easy for the AS partner to misinterpret non-verbal behaviour or body language. When unsure, it is important to ask the neurotypical partner, for example, what a look means, saying, 'Why are you looking at me like that?'. The neurotypical partner then asks, 'What do you think it means?'. The AS partner then answers and hopefully a discussion takes place, where misunderstandings can be avoided and both partners learn more about each other.
- *Rules for socialising*. It is sometimes helpful if the couple have a prearranged agreement or series of coded signs for communication when socialising. So, for example, a pinch or a movement of finger to lip might mean, 'Stop saying what you are saying immediately'. A wink might mean, 'You are doing very well'. If the AS person is feeling overloaded by the situation, they could say, 'I think I have a migraine coming on', as an excuse to leave.

8 The effect of diagnosis on marriage and romantic partnerships

A diagnosis not only affects the persons themselves but most of the relationships the persons are in. In romantic partnerships or marriages, where one member has AS and the other is neurotypical, reactions can vary. The general consensus seems to be that a diagnosis represents a positive change aiding understanding, improving coping and strengthening the relationship. However, on rarer occasions the diagnosis might not make the relationship stronger. Here follows two different stories from neurotypical partners and their different reactions to their partners getting a diagnosis of AS.

Michael, married to Gill who obtained a late-in-life AS diagnosis, tells his story:

> Before getting the diagnosis, we'd been married for five years and used to have lots of arguments. The diagnosis has helped me understand Gill more and we've gradually worked it out. When we used to get into a conversation about emotions Gill would stop talking, start to pace up and down, cry and wring her hands. I would get angry with her and say something cruel like, 'Grow up, you're an adult' and sometimes walk out slamming the door. Now I know she just can't process emotions the way other people do. I say to myself, 'She can't help it', and stay calm. I then try to explain in a calm rational manner because that makes sense to Gill. Sometimes she needs to type an answer and we will sit on the sofa texting each other. I also now know Gill needs a set routine in the morning. Everything has to be done the same way. I don't speak to her for the first 20 minutes; then I'll bring her a cup of coffee just as she likes it. Now that I know how her mind works I can appreciate it – she communicates rationally in logic and fact. I love her for the way she is, different from everybody else. She's unique, brilliant and honest and I believe we challenge each other and are growing into better people.

A different story comes from Vanessa, a neurotypical lady married to Alan, who obtained a diagnosis three years ago:

> I must say getting the diagnosis for Alan was a turning point for me and our 15-year marriage, which has always been difficult. For Alan it was brilliant, a validation of the way he was, but I began to see him as a different person. I began to see more and more how he was preoccupied with his work and his hobbies and I felt neglected and unloved. When pushed he would show some affection but I knew he was only going through the motions. I don't think he really felt it. I realised that he would never change. His brain was wired up logically and I know he loved me in his rational way and was totally loyal, but I'm more emotional and our worlds were drifting apart. The more I became depressed the more he failed to connect with me. What made it worse was that I could see our son, who also has AS, slowly changing and becoming more empathic,

with the help he was getting at school, but Alan wasn't. I started chatting to a male friend at work who was going through a divorce and I realised that a man could be emotional and sensitive. This has created problems because I feel torn.

9 Sexuality

There are issues around sexuality for people on the autism spectrum. A research study comparing 50 people with an ASD and 53 matched controls indicated generally lower libido reported among both males and female ASD participants. There were also higher rates of 'tomboyism', 'bisexuality' and 'asexuality' in the female ASD group. For men, particularly young men, the issue might be trying to find a sexual partner, where poor social skills, difficulty communicating, flirting, 'reading signals' and maintaining a relationship can be a problem, resulting in real frustration.

For AS women, married to a neurotypical man, there might be potential problems. One married lady with AS commented: 'I'm not really interested in sex and don't really want it. But my logical brain says I should be doing it to keep my husband happy.' A proportion of people with AS are not interested in an intimate relationship or a sexual relationship. Emma, a recently diagnosed 30-year-old, commented: 'I'm asexual and aromantic. I don't feel sexual or romantic feelings. In fact I'm repulsed.' Temple Grandin said, 'My sense of self and happiness is tied up with what I do, my career and I don't need or want an intimate sexual relationship'. Tony Attwood suggested in a recent presentation, in Berkshire, the interesting thought that in Europe a thousand years ago, many of the monasteries, where they found pleasure in routine, solitary activities, and celibacy, were probably full of people with AS!

Chapter Ten

Problems with co-morbid mental health

1 Neurological and psychiatric overlapping diagnosis (co-morbidities)

AS overlaps with a number of other neurological and psychiatric conditions. Those neurological or neurodevelopmental conditions, where the primary problem is the wiring of the brain, include Attention Deficit Hyperactivity Disorder (ADHD), dyslexia, dyspraxia, dyscalculia, Tourette's syndrome and epilepsy. On top of these shared conditions the child with autism is 2–6 times at greater risk of experiencing co-morbid psychiatric conditions than their normal peers. People with AS are more vulnerable to secondary mental health conditions, such as anxiety, depression, low self-esteem, obsessive compulsive disorder (OCD), eating disorders, psychosis, bipolar disorder and personality

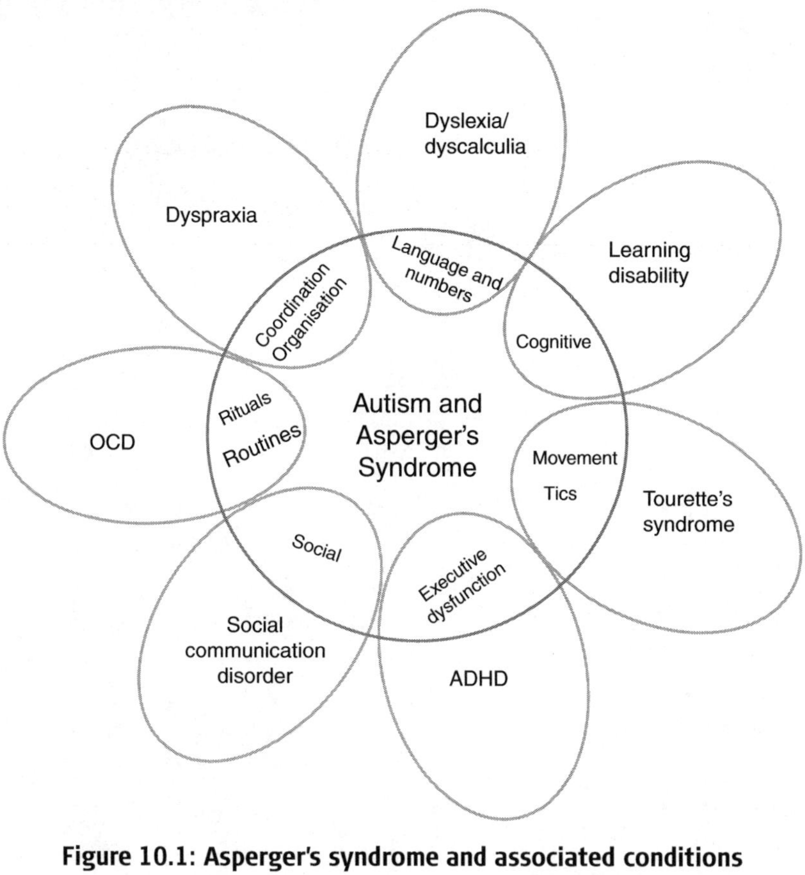

Figure 10.1: Asperger's syndrome and associated conditions

disorders. It is easy to imagine how the social, emotional, behavioural and sensory struggles of living with AS can often lead to secondary mental health problems. It is estimated that 15–20% of long term users of adult mental health services have diagnosed or undiagnosed AS. There is also the problem of individuals being misdiagnosed with other psychiatric conditions such as schizophrenia or borderline personality disorder or bipolar disorder, when the underlying problem is AS.

There are a few factors that can influence the likelihood of having mental health problems alongside AS. These include the following:

(a) Whether the diagnosis has occurred early in life, the level of understanding about this condition and what post diagnostic support was received.
(b) The demands of the social and emotional environment the person is in and the level of support, including the level of isolation.
(c) The demands of the sensory environment – factors such as the noise level that may cause distress and increase stress levels.
(d) The amount of teasing, bullying and trauma experienced in earlier life and its effect on self-esteem.

2 Primary neurodevelopmental co-morbidities

(a) ADHD. The most common co-morbidity with AS is ADHD, sometimes presenting in a less active form as attention deficit disorder (ADD), without the hyperactivity. The general condition of ADHD comprises between 3 and 5 per cent of the general population. The characteristics are hyperactivity, which means being fidgety, 'on the go', restless, finding it difficult to relax, often being impulsive, acting before thinking and having difficulty concentrating, filtering out background information and splitting and dividing attention. People with ADHD get bored very easily, need a high level of stimulation and can be forgetful and disorganised, often talking excessively. Approximately 10 per cent of people with AS would meet the criteria for ADHD or ADD. When people have both conditions, the results can be quite disabling. Marjorie characterised it by saying,

> 'It's like there are two voices in my head; one wants me to be obsessive and develop special interests and really focus on something, but the other is restless and pulls me away – I just don't have the patience to develop an all-encompassing special interest'.

People with subclinical levels of both AS and ADHD are at a real disadvantage, because the combination of these difficulties means they have very real problems, but because they don't have enough symptoms of either, they sometimes miss out on a full diagnosis.

(b) Dyspraxia. This is a condition, sometimes known as 'developmental coordination disorder', characterised by poor gross and fine motor skills, poor eye–hand coordination and clumsiness. As a child there are often marked delays in learning to walk, poor ball skills, poor coordination with tasks such as riding a bicycle, tying a knot in a tie or a bow in shoelaces and often poor handwriting. These motor difficulties are often coupled with poor executive abilities, difficulties with memory and organization and problems learning and carrying out sequences. Approximately 90 per cent of people with dyspraxia have another neurodevelopmental disorder such as AS or ADHD.

(c) Tourette's syndrome. Prevalence rates are estimated as being between 0.15 and 1.8 per cent of the general population. The condition is characterised by a tic, which is an involuntary, rapid, recurrent non-rhythmic motor or vocal action. It is sudden and purposeless. Research suggests that between 20 and 60 per cent of children with AS develop tics. About 10 per cent of people with autism have vocal or motor tics. Simple tics can include eye blinking or rolling, facial grimacing, shoulder shrugging, tongue protrusions, knuckle cracking, throat clearing, grunting and making different meaningless sounds. More complex tics might include gyrating, touching objects, swearing or repeating certain words or phrases. Between 20 and 60 per cent of people with AS have tics or involuntary, repetitive contractions of groups of muscles, including vocal cords. In AS tics tend to wax and wane with degrees of stress and depression.

(d) Dyslexia/Hyperlexia. Dyslexia is defined as having difficulty with literacy or words which might include reading, spelling and writing. People with dyslexia often have problems with working memory (the ability to retain information over a very short period of time, often a matter of seconds), for a series of unconnected items, which might be letters, numbers or sounds. The opposite of dyslexia is hyperlexia meaning a superability or precocious ability to read and decode words often without understanding their meaning. Both dyslexia and hyperlexia are common in AS. One study suggested 5–10% of autistic children were hyperlexic.

(e) Dyscalculia. While the majority of people with AS are proficient with numbers and figures, some are very poor and simply can't do arithmetic taking years to learn to add, subtract, divide and multiply or tell the time or have an awareness of time. Some people with autism really struggle with the concept of time and placing events chronologically while others are exceptionally good

(f) Epilepsy. One in four children with autism has a seizure disorder. Seizures can range from full-scale convulsions to brief staring spells. Little is known about the prevalence in the milder condition of Asperger's.

(g) Learning disability (LD). A high proportion of people with very severe autism have an LD; research suggests this is as high as 50 per cent. By definition, AS is a milder degree of autism, where the person is average or above-average intelligence and by definition does not have a learning disability. However, a proportion of people with AS get misdiagnosed as having an LD, but actually just have an unusual cognitive profile, being very strong on certain thing and very weak at others.

3 Secondary psychiatric difficulties

(a) Anxiety

Experiencing anxiety is by far the most common and highest rated problem for people with AS, because of at least four major root causes: (1) difficulty socialising with continuous possibility of making mistakes and feeling humiliated; (2) the stress of coping with unpredictability, random events and changes to routine; (3) the stress of sensory experiences and sensory overload such as too much overwhelming noise, light, smell; and (4) special fears or phobias such as telephones, the dark or large dogs.

Experiencing anxiety is a vicious circle as the more anxious a person feels, the more they tighten up and become rigid, the more socialising becomes difficult and the more sensory issues impinge. Then the person avoids, escapes or doesn't cope, which creates more anxiety next time around, resulting in a negative feedback loop, an escalation or a vicious circle. Typical ways of coping with anxiety might include: (1) escape, avoidance, refusal, social phobia and solitude; (2) engaging in routine and rituals in an attempt to make the world more controllable and predictable; (3) taking prescription medication, alcohol and drugs; (4) freezing – selective mutism; (5) engaging in special interests, where the person feels more in control; and (6) storing up and having 'meltdowns'. Most of these strategies produce short-term benefits in relief from anxiety, but have the potential to store up added long-term difficulties. Part of the problem for people with AS is that they are very anxious but are not always aware of the negative automatic thoughts or triggers that create that anxiety. It is hard for the person with AS to identify the 'cognitive' or thinking component or anxiety.

The condition of 'social anxiety' or 'social phobia' in neurotypical people is similar but different from that experienced by people with AS. However, the difference between the two conditions is that someone with social anxiety has only a mild social skill deficit and an excessive amount of avoidance and anxiety, whereas the person with AS often has a much bigger social skill deficit, that is, they lack the social skills to have a successful social interaction and therefore avoidance is used as an adaptive strategy.

Tips for coping with anxiety

- Try to work out what triggers and causes your anxiety. Write a list so you will be able to anticipate and plan for situations.
- Have a place to go, a sanctuary or retreat, where there is minimum stimulation where you can be alone and de-stress.
- Take care of yourself with a good diet, plenty of sleep and exercise that raises your heartbeat.
- Learn a relaxation technique such as mindfulness or breathing exercises. Try to fill your mind with a soothing picture.
- Immerse yourself in your special interest.
- Learn to forgive yourself for your mistakes – no one is perfect. Focus on your strong points.

(b) Depression

In AS depression is sometimes experienced in an unconventional way because the person has difficulty understanding and expressing emotions and may not hang on to lingering unhappy emotions from the past. Rather than a prolonged period of sustained gloom the person might have a briefer 'depression attack', rather like a panic attack, which can come quickly, be intense and overwhelming, and then go quickly. The person is vulnerable to suicidal thoughts, self-harm and even suicide. This is an emotion where there can be an extreme of absolute hopelessness, nothing in between and no grey areas.

People with AS are prone to depression for several reasons. They are likely to have low self-esteem from a history of feeling different, being bullied and failing in social and occupational situations. They may experience loneliness, isolation and lack of support, with an inbuilt tendency to find sharing and communicating feelings difficult. They are often perfectionists, liking to get things just right and noticing any mistakes, which can precipitate a sense of failure. Furthermore, nuerotypicals can often lift their mood by talking to friends, going out or using humour, whereas, in contrast, people with AS often have difficulty resonating with and infusing the happiness from others. A recent research study by Cassidy et al (2014) indicated that people diagnosed with AS are more prone to suicidal ideation and suicidal thoughts than the general population and have more potential risk factors for secondary depression.

Some people with AS seem to have generally low capacity for pleasure and reward in life. The pleasure and reward areas of their brains involving the dopamine pathways are simply not as active. There is a condition called 'anhedonia', which means, 'the inability to experience pleasure from activity usually found enjoyable, such as eating, exercise, social interaction and sexual experiences'. Some people with AS say they experience anhedonia, although others say they get a great deal of pleasure from their special interests and a few more say they experience pleasure but not from social situations. Thomas's story illustrates this point:

> I don't have needs or an appetite; everything is a means to an end. I'll be glad when it's all over. My wife said let's go on holiday and I think, 'why, what's the point'. I do things to make my wife happy. I try to be a good provider and husband – and I suppose that is a sort of vicarious pleasure, but I don't need any of it. I never look forward to anything whether it be a new car, birthday, holiday or Christmas ... it's just another day. I have no needs for friends. Social interaction is like a game which I will play for a while and then come home and play with my cars. I don't get any pleasure out of physical contact. Linda says let's have a cuddle on the settee and I think, what for?

Tips for coping with depression

- Know yourself. Simply knowing about AS can make sense of years of frustration and baffling failure.
- Stop blaming yourself. One man said: 'The more I understand about Asperger's the more I realise it's not my fault ... my brain is just wired up differently.'
- Keep busy and have routines and interests. Immersing yourself in a special interest or taking on a caring role for others shifts your attention away from negative self-pitying thoughts.
- Understand and express yourself through music, art or creative channels
- Ensure you allot time for exercise, good diet and communing with nature
- Develop a spiritual interest – an awareness of a higher purpose putting self into context.
- Seek the help of medication: Temple Grandin says that she takes a low dose of an antidepressant which stops her constant anxiety and panic attacks.
- Consider seeking professional help

(c) Low self-esteem

People with AS often have problems with low self-esteem because they felt different growing up, experiencing bullying, criticism from peers, lack of friends and self-criticism from making mistakes. Paul said: 'I've always felt different, like I'm not good enough. I try to keep below the radar, be unnoticed, but I've still been bullied, harassed, shunned, rejected and ostracised. People want to know what's wrong with me. I want to know too.'

Tips for coping with poor self-esteem

- Accept that difference is not defective. Accepting yourself just as you are makes it more likely that others will accept you.

- Write two lists. In the first, think of aspects about yourself that you are proud of or that people have complimented you on, for example, your honesty and your loyalty. Then, in the second list, identify your abilities or things that you are good at, for example, memory or eye for detail. It may help to ask family and friends to help you complete the list.
- Remind yourself that you are doing your best and that you are not a 'bad person'. Stop and remind yourself when being bullied: 'Who really is the lesser person, me the victim? Or the predator?'.
- Find like-minded people who have similar interests or characteristics like you. There may be a group of people who also go to 'Dr Who' or 'Star Trek' conventions and play the same computer games.
- Spend time with nature, animals or pets. People with AS often have special abilities to commune with animals, which can be a great boost to self-esteem because they are often genuinely pleased to see you, show affection and are non-judgemental.
- Identify the value of being different. Some of the greatest advances in science and the arts have been achieved by people who were different and some of whom had autistic traits. Read about AS achievers such as Albert Einstein, Alan Turing and Mozart.

(d) Schizophrenia or psychosis

True schizophrenia is uncommon in people with AS, although because of the shared history of the two conditions, there is often some confusion. Individuals with AS have a marginally higher chance of developing psychosis than the average person with less than 4 per cent developing signs of schizophrenia. A small minority of young adults can develop genuine signs of schizophrenia, such as hearing voices or paranoia, but such episodes tend to be brief and often linked to a particularly stressful event. Many individuals get wrongly diagnosed as having schizophrenia because some symptoms of AS, such as poor social communication skills, unusual thinking, self-neglect and bizarre behaviour, resemble the negative symptoms and disorganised thinking and behaviour of schizophrenia. Some adolescents with AS can show a temporary deterioration in ability, increased social withdrawal, lack of concern for personal hygiene and an intense preoccupation with their interests. They might vocalise their thoughts or talk about themselves in the third person or be suspicious of others. A lack of ToM can also resemble paranoia in some cases. One obvious differentiating factor is that for a diagnosis of schizophrenia there is a progressive loss of social contact but for an ASD there never has been extensive social contact.

Jeffery's story seems relevant:

> I was bullied excessively at school, had a breakdown and became reclusive for three years and only then got a diagnosis of Asperger's syndrome. I have been sectioned and had a number of admissions to psychiatric hospitals over the years and now take a small dose of antipsychotic medication. I think my parents and the police overreact – I'm not psychotic. I'm just having a massive meltdown and get paranoid. Ever since I was a child I have hated loud noises or people banging things and can get quite paranoid about it. Recently we had a big family Christmas meal with about 12 people – I was already stressed beforehand. There were lots of little sub-conversations and my sister was banging things down on the table and I thought she was doing it deliberately. I stood up in the middle of the meal and started shouting and punched myself in the eye and ran off. I get paranoid about a number of things. For example, I often think my neighbour is deliberately making noise to get back at me or if people are sniffing or coughing in public I think they are doing that to wind me up. This year I planned Christmas better so that I saw everybody individually or in small groups, with a gap between meetings, so I didn't have to sit down to one of those big family meals. I have learned to get into the habit of swimming every day and after 20 lengths I'm a different person, much calmer.

(e) Borderline personality disorder (BPD)

Research by Lugnegard and colleagues, in 2011, identified 54 adults clinically diagnosed with AS, and approximately half of these fulfilled the criteria for personality disorder. The diagnosis BPD, often referred to as 'emotional regulation disorder,' and AS have considerable overlaps, and there are frequent misdiagnoses and misunderstandings between the two conditions. A cardinal characteristic of BPD is a poor attachment early in life which can result in symptoms similar to AS. Both groups might have severe mood swings or 'meltdowns' characterised by rage. Both can also have very 'black-and-white thinking' or 'splitting' where something is seen as completely good or completely bad, with the tendency to either idolise or vilify people. Both can also be self-centred, showing low empathy when in a mood and oblivious to the hurt they may cause to those closest to them. Both can have stormy, difficult relationships and poor attachment styles. Both groups have an above-average number of suicidal thoughts and tendency to self-harm. There are also issues around self-identity for both groups. There is also a higher than average rate of childhood, physical and sexual abuse and bullying within both groups. The following are the differentiators:

- The person with BPD knows how to make friends, and has good social skills, but has difficulty keeping relationships, often having arguments and falling out, whereas the person with AS has more difficulty making friends.
- The person with AS often has a 'low openness to new practical and emotional experiences', meaning, they are not novelty or change seekers, but prefer sameness and routine, whereas the person with BPD often seeks change 'stimulation' and new experiences.
- The person with AS is more likely to have communication difficulties with the literal use of language, difficulty interpreting non-verbal behaviour and problems with the pragmatic use of language.

- The person with AS is more likely to have hardwired sensory sensitivities (noise, light, touch, taste etc) and motor coordination problems.
- Self-harm in BPD is often due to interpersonal reasons such as being angry with someone, feeling rejected, or trying to get someone's attention, whereas in AS self-harm is often due to a combination of overloads of sensory, social, cognitive systems and is often carefully planned and systematic, rather than impulsive and chaotic.
- The person with AS is often straightforward, honest, dutiful with a frankness in expression, often adhering to the rules, with a tendency to think things through before acting, whereas the person with BPD is often more impulsive and less straightforward.
- The person with BPD is often very sensitive to criticism and is highly sensitive to interpreting events as being signs of rejection and abandonment, whereas the person with AS is often less sensitive or emotionally reactive to criticism. One extreme example of this was Arthur, a very rational, logical man with AS, who made the following enlightening comments: 'I don't like praise or words of affection about my good points because I know all that. I'd prefer criticism, because it's something I don't know and I can learn from.'
- The person with AS might have the ability to hyperfocus and tend to become immersed in obsessive special interests and routines.

Ingrid had problems in relationships, particularly with her parents. She was socially isolated, emotionally unstable, often flying into rages, and was rather prone to 'black-and-white' thinking. The local community mental health team diagnosed her as having a BPD. She was eventually referred for an assessment of AS where one comment she made gave a decisive clue towards supporting an AS rather than BPD diagnosis. Ingrid said:

> When I was a child, my mother tried to help me, encouraging me to look at people rather than avoid eye contact. She also taught me how to cope better with social situations by understanding trick questions. She

> said people will say to you, 'Do you like my jumper?'. My mother told me not to always tell the truth, because other people don't always want the truth; these are trick questions. Since then I have tried to pick out trick questions and not take things so literally.

There is a high rate of people with underlying AS being misdiagnosed with BPD, and getting a correct diagnosis can often helpfully change the emphasis of psychological treatment. There are, however, some people who may have an underlying AS condition and have significant secondary traits of BPD.

(f) Obsessive compulsive disorder (OCD)

There are many similarities between an ASD and OCD as both involve having rigid repetitive actions and routines and a narrow range of repetitive thoughts about a subject. People with OCD and AS often have difficulty tolerating uncertainty and a tendency towards concrete thinking style. Research suggests that between 8 and 20 per cent of people with AS have a co-diagnosis of OCD. However, there are differences between the routines, rituals and compulsions of AS and that of OCD. The main difference is that in OCD the intrusive, invasive thoughts are not welcome or wanted and bring enormous anxiety, which triggers a compulsive activity to neutralise the thought and reduce the anxiety – termed 'egodystonic'. In AS the thoughts are quite pleasurable and the person does not have a desire to resist or stop having the thought – they are not coated with anxiety. The thoughts and repetitive activities might be part of a special interest and bring inherent pleasure and are not there to reduce anxiety. It is the function of the repetitive compulsive patterns which are different in both conditions.

People with AS are likely to display compulsions related to hoarding or repetitive ordering, touching or tapping or sexual obsessions whereas individuals with OCD are more likely to have obsessions surrounding cleaning or contamination themes with compulsions related to counting, washing or checking. People with AS may have a particular vulnerability to develop a fixed idea, or distressing preoccupation, about a part of their body, which is known as body dysmorphia and is a type of OCD.

(g) Eating disorders

People with AS are at risk of developing eating disorders. Professor Janet Treasure (2013) reports that 20 per cent of an eating disorder sample had AS. She points out that people with AS, particularly high-functioning females, are at very high risk for developing an eating disorder because of the following:

- AS people like to focus on the details of food and weight.
- Once they have learned a rule they find it difficult to shift.
- There is an inability to focus on the bigger picture, to see the wood from the trees – lack of central coherence.
- There is also a weak ToM or difficulty working out how other people might perceive the person and their weight or body image.
- There are perfectionistic traits, and sometimes food and weight can become a 'special interest'.

(h) Bipolar disorder

Bipolar disorder is a psychiatric condition previously known as manic depression, characterised by fluctuating and rapidly cycling moods, from elation to despair. A small number of people with AS have co-morbid bipolar disorder, but misdiagnosis is common. Many people with AS, with a tendency to view the world through rather 'black and white', 'all or nothing', 'good or bad' filters find that their mood can very quickly spiral downwards or even upwards. There is not much middle ground in between the extremes. However, it is also important not to confuse AS over excitement over a special interest with mania.

4 Tips for clients and staff working in a hospital

For clients:

- Take an emergency comfort pack (headphones, music, sunglasses etc).
- Try to explain to people about your AS and special needs.
- Identify the quietest room on the ward and make use of it.
- Identify the triggers that make you nervous and uncomfortable and tell staff.
- Avoid incidents involving other people's emotional disturbance – don't get involved.

For staff:

- Accept that the person with AS will often have poor eye contact, will not be sociable and may appear abrupt.
- Bear in mind that people with AS like structure, routine, order and predictability and don't like changes. They like to know what is coming, so having a plan or timetable may help.
- People with AS do not like to be socially overstimulated – a psychiatric ward might feel like the worst place in the world for them! They need to be on their own.
- Remember that they may have sensory sensitivities – show them a quiet room on the ward and be aware of lighting, smells and overcrowding. Make reasonable allowances to their requests.
- Individuals with AS like to understand what is going on and the reason for things, so try to keep them involved. They might keep asking questions. Explain and keep explaining.
- Use visual timetables. Write things down, even if it is only key words on a white board.
- Be patient; take time; don't rush the person.

- Avoid making flippant comments. Be aware that the person might not know when you are joking.
- Use simple direct language. Try to avoid open-ended questions such as, 'How do you feel?'. Use visual anxiety scales so that the patient can indicate how anxious he or she is.
- Find out what the patient likes to do – their special interests and make sure this is available to them.

Chapter Eleven

Autism and the criminal justice system

1 Introduction

The overwhelming majority of people with AS are law-abiding citizens, often with very clear conventional ideas about what is right or wrong. However, when crimes occur, such as mass killings, often committed by a loner, such as Martin Bryant in Australia or Adam Lanza in the US, there has tended to be the cry of 'He's on the spectrum' often made by laypeople. When the cases are looked at in more detail, it is apparent that a pre-crime diagnosis has not been made, retrospective diagnosis is often ambivalent, and there are often a variety of other personality and psychiatric factors to take into account. However, young people with AS are more likely than the neurotypical population to enter the criminal justice system . To understand the link between Asperger's and crime, it is important to examine the type of offences and the reason for these offences. This chapter will discuss the four main types of offending behaviour in individuals with AS.

2 Problems created by lack of understanding or naivety

Many individuals with AS find that problems are created by lack of understanding, misinterpretation of social cues, social naivety or immaturity. One scenario might involve inappropriate social behaviours which are interpreted as unwanted sexual advances. These may be reported as a crime or difficulty judging ages of others which may lead to sexual offences with a minor. When in custody, individuals with AS are often quick to confess and justify their actions, perhaps not being able to understand what all the fuss is about – they view their actions as logical, justified and appropriate without any associated emotion or remorse. However, there are cases of young women with AS, particularly in residential care, whose social vulnerability has been exploited so that unfortunately they have been sexually abused by predatory male staff. Similarly, online, internet interactions can leave vulnerable young AS women in positions where they are 'groomed', exploited and abused. One mother said: 'Jackie doesn't have a concept of danger, is much too trusting and is frankly at risk. If she's known somebody online for a week she thinks they are her new best friend. She has got into cars with men and naïvely arranged to meet a man in his forties and she is only 19.'

3 Problems arising from disruption to routine

Aggressive behaviour can arise from a disruption to routine, stress from changing a daily routine or from sensory overload. This kind of aggressive behaviour is a reaction of frustration and aggression to a situation of stress or arousal rather than instrumental aggression. People with AS are often less aware of a gradual build-up of stress and just explode. One man was very sensitive to the noise of a neighbour's dog barking and decided to take the law into his own hands. He became verbally and physically aggressive towards the neighbour who ended up reporting him to the police. His desire for justice in his problem situation overrode other considerations.

4 Problems occurring from preoccupation with a special interest

In some situations, preoccupation with a special interest may lead to an offence. In one case a man with a special interest in tractors stole a tractor that had no practical use and could not have been sold for financial gain. The compulsive nature of the special interest was so strong the man was tempted to commit an offence without thinking through the consequences. Another man developed a special interest in the transport system and was charged with impersonating a bus driver. Obsessive interests, or rituals, may develop into a dangerous action.

Gary McKinnon was a young British man, with AS, who hacked into the computer system of the US government from his bedroom in his parents' home in North London. He had developed a remarkably high level of computer skill and became quite obsessed with this special interest and finding out what information the Pentagon kept on its computers. He was socially isolated and showed significant social naïveté that he did not comprehend that he had committed a crime or the consequences of his actions. He did not attempt to hide his crime and left notes on each computer saying that he had been there. He seemed unable to imagine that the authorities would view his behaviour as criminal or what the social consequences would be. The Americans wanted him extradited and to stand trial for his 'crime' but thankfully the UK authorities recognised that Gary had Asperger's and decided that the threat of prison was a sufficient deterrent to reduce the risk of similar occurrences. His neurological condition was eventually treated with dignity and compassion. This illustrates how Gary's computer skills and special interest were impressive, but those very skills and interests became unacceptable in a certain context which Gary did not recognise as significant due to his AS.

5 Problems associated with vulnerability and court

Individuals with AS are often vulnerable to exploitation by others because they don't understand hidden meanings and intentions. They may be used as scapegoats in crimes when actually they are not to blame. When in custody, they may be more likely to be suggestible. If they are finding the interrogation particularly unpleasant, due to lack of familiarity, loud noises, lack of understanding or hostility, they may be inclined to admit to the crime just so they can remove themselves from the situation. Giving evidence in court can be particularly stressful to those with AS. Many AS individuals, particularly when cross-questioned, may react very angrily to any insinuation that they have lied and thereby appear more pervasively angry, confrontational and anti-social than they actually are. They may have a lot of difficulty understanding the language of the courtroom, for example, figures of speech such as 'Bear with me', 'Set me straight', 'Not in any way, shape or form' or 'I'm going to jog your memory'. They may not understand why they are being asked the same questions a number of times. They have extreme difficulty in answering questions which involve having an understanding of what another person's intention is.

Anxiety may prevent people with AS from being able to process the questions that they are being asked. These difficulties make witnesses or suspects more vulnerable and they may be eligible for the intermediary scheme. The intermediary's function is to communicate to the vulnerable witness, explain difficult questions and recommend calming measures such as frequent breaks if necessary.

Chapter Twelve

Special interests

1 Development of special interests

People with AS have a great ability to develop special, narrow, obsessive interests, which often involve an accumulation and categorisation of knowledge and facts about a particular area. These interests, according to the diagnostic textbooks, are an 'encompassing preoccupation or restricted patterns of interest that are abnormal in either intensity or focus'. The clinician has to make a subjective judgement about how extreme the interest is, whether it is just an excessive hobby or if there is a repetitive adherence, consuming enormous time, disrupting daily life and limiting the person's social opportunities. A special interest is a form of systematising, collecting information and facts, understanding the rules of how things work, spotting patterns, distinguishing between types. The interest might be a mechanical system (an engine or computer game), a natural system (the weather or animals), a numerical system (timetables, calendars, finance or coding/programming), a collectable system (rocks, cards and badges), language system (learning a language) or a movement system (martial arts, dance, running). Unusual or special interests can develop very early in life – as young as two years. Sometimes it might commence with spinning the wheels of a toy car, lining up toys or collecting coins or pencils or Thomas the Tank Engine. The attachment to the objects can be very intense. It is almost as if the social and interpersonal world can be difficult and confusing but here is something that is calming and soothing that can be controlled. The interest is often solitary. One mother recalled:

> Jamie could draw amazingly well even at the age of two or three years. He would draw an apple with a little leaf coming off it or a person with all the details such as fingers, toes and the body would be in perfect proportion ... he has continued to be obsessive about art and has just completed his degree.

In the pre-teens and teenagers, the interests often include computers, electronics or computer games, science fiction or fantasy or people, or characters real or fictional.

2 Collections and categories

The person may become an avid collector, and as the collection increases, the person develops a cataloguing system almost like a library – the system having subsystems that are often very ordered. David said: 'When I was younger I used to collect comics and keep them in neat piles on the shelves in my bedroom and I'd read them over and over. On one occasion I noticed that a story line had been repeated two years after it first appeared and so I wrote to the comic. They replied apologising, but then they did it again.' The collection of objects and facts can develop into real expertise. Facts give comfort and security. Popular interests now are different as fashions change. For example, Thomas the Tank Engine, Dinosaurs, Fossils, Pokémon cards, Lego trains and cars have been replaced with computer games and Japanese cartoons. Girls seem to have less obvious special interests than boys and these might include animals, particularly horses, or the science fiction books about Harry Potter. Indeed Harry Potter was a bit of an outcast who turns into a triumphant hero, a figure with magical power – a figure people with AS can identify with easily. Girls often tend to watch soap operas on TV partly as a way of learning about social relationships.

Common special interests	
Transport/mechanical	Trains, planes, ships, cars, tractors, buses, Thomas the Tank Engine, washing machines, lawn mowers, maps, road systems
Science	Mathematics, coding/programming, engineering, fossils, global warming, geology, timetables, weather
Pets/animals	Horses, dinosaurs
Strategic games	Computer games, online role-playing games
Creative/artistic interests	Music, art, writing, language
Comics/cartoons	Anime, Manga, Marvel and DC comics
Films/books/TV	*Harry Potter, Lord of the Rings, Star Wars, Star Trek, Dr Who*, ghosts, fantasy, UFOs, science fiction, crime, Disney, Red Dwarf.

(*continued*)

(*continued*)

Collections	Pokémon cards, badges, sparkly things, matchbox cars, Lego, shiny things, bottles, rocks, My Little Pony, sports statistics
Martial arts/sports	Taekwondo, formula one, running, cycling, archery, chess
History	First World War, Second World War, Vikings, Egyptians
People	Sherlock Holmes, James Bond, Bertie Wooster, politicians, pop stars
Less common interests	Cars made by the Rootes Motor Group, Mississippi Hill Country Blues

3 Function of the special interest

Once the interest is developed in times of stress or chaos, it can be enormously soothing, relaxing and calming because it is predictable, regular, ordered and secure. The repetitive nature of the interest can reduce feelings of stress. People with AS might find the world chaotic, focusing on details and not be able to see the 'big picture or the general coherence'. The interest offers a sense of coherence, predictability and certainty in life. One man said: 'The world is chaotic, frightening and disorganised, but organising something like my rock collection helps me shake off that feeling of chaos that comes from living in such a frightening disorganised world.' Often the more stressed the person's life the more pronounced the special interest becomes. The special interest is also enormously pleasurable experience often greater than many other pleasures in life. The person has found something more pleasurable than socialising. It allows a development of expertise, boosts self-esteem, provides something to talk about, provides an identity and sometimes can create friendships. Often a person with AS will define a friend as 'someone with similar interests'. It also offers the opportunity to escape into an alternative world.

4 The reaction of others

The capacity to talk endlessly about the subject can be a real strain for the rest of the family. The recollection of an elder sister to her AS brother is typical: 'For years all my brother would talk about at the dinner table was bionicles (a type of Lego). I used to feel so angry I would sometimes shout at him. He couldn't conceive that anybody would want to talk about anything else. He still got them lined up in his room 15 years later.' People with AS often describe the overwhelming desire to talk about the subject whether or not anybody was interested and often in a monologue: 'I don't care whether they are interested or bored I wanted to talk about it. It was like a spring within me that had to get out.' The notion that people with AS have impaired executive skills and often a one-track mind fits in with this as it is almost as if they lack the ability and will to switch attention, and change track. During the diagnostic assessment the clinician might notice the client come to life and be more animated when talking about their special interest. The key skill for the person with AS is to know when to and when not to speak about their special interest. Some people rely on a partner or family member to give a special secret sign, such as a hand signal, which means, 'You've said enough; reel it in; stop talking about it; the other person is not interested.'

5 Developing the interest into a job

It is possible that some special interests become sources of employment. For example, a person interested in planes can become a cabin crew, one who is interested in computers can become an IT specialist, a person interested in computer games can become a computer games designer, one who has interest in insects can become an entomologist and so on.

Chapter Thirteen

Work

1 An underused employment resource

In the UK, the percentage of adults with autism (ASCs) in full-time employment is estimated to be about 15%, in part-time employment about 9% and the proportion of unemployed graduates about 26% (National Autistic Society, 2009). Two further points are worth considering; (1), most individuals with AS who are unemployed wish to work – it is a waste of a good resource if they are unemployed – and (2), around one-third of those who do work experience bullying or discrimination as a result of their condition. If people with AS can find a welcoming niche, or the right circumstances, they can be extremely successful because they have the valuable skills needed.

If people with AS can be accommodated within a job by their employer, they tend to stay. They are often loyal, although this is often interpreted as a love of stability. One man, who is a researcher at a university, commented: 'I don't want to move from this job unless I'm forced to. I'm happy to do it for the rest of my life; even when I retire I'll probably still keep coming to the campus as a volunteer.' Having a stable workforce is highly beneficial for the company.

2 Who is there to help?

There is growing recognition of the value of employment support agencies in helping people with AS find work, write curriculum vitae, cope with an interview and explain to prospective employers something about the needs of a person with AS. There are some employment schemes through which companies have sought out or positively discriminated in favour of people with AS. One such was a Danish company called The Specialists that tested electronic equipment such as computer programs and new telephone systems. This was managed by a man with a child with autism who actively sought out employees with AS because of their eye for detail and enjoyment of repetitive tasks. Other larger international IT companies have a considerable percentage of staff with undiagnosed AS. German software giant SAP hopes to recruit hundreds of people with AS. The chief executive of SAP comments: 'Only by employing people who think differently and spark innovation will SAP be prepared to handle the challenges of the twenty-first century ... innovation comes from the edges.'

3 Know both your strengths and weaknesses

Understanding how the AS brain works is the most valuable thing a person can do to boost their career and live a rewarding life. An attention to detail and the ability to hyperfocus on one particular thing is one strength individuals with AS possess. Nick comments: 'When I focus on writing a programme I forget to eat, drink and go to the bathroom I'm so engrossed. All I need is a computer and a bed.' Scientists and artists often have an overpowering obsession that allows them to immerse themselves completely in their work that they forget all other distractions.

In contrast, one weakness individuals with AS often have is poor 'executive functioning', that is, skills such as being able to stand back and 'see the big picture', to plan and organise, multitask, prioritise and divide and switch attention from one task to another. A further weakness might be prolonged face-to-face interaction, which requires good social skills and a pleasure in socialising. To identify strengths and weaknesses a vocational assessment with an independent professional would be ideal, looking at cognitive abilities, personality, motivation, interests and interpersonal skills. However, finding an occupational psychologist with a good knowledge of AS might not be easy. So the assessment of the person's profile of skills might have to be done with a close family member or friend or by making an accurate appraisal by self-reflection and looking in the mirror. What is the person good at, interested in, what are the likely problems that need to be anticipated? A good exercise is to sit down with somebody who knows you well and draw up a list of strengths and weaknesses.

4 Positive and negative qualities of people with Asperger's syndrome in the workplace

Positive qualities of people with AS in the workplace are as follows:

- Reliable and hard working – conscientious wants to 'do a good job'.
- Perfectionistic – accurate, good at identifying errors, eye for detail, likes to 'get it right'.
- Persistent – likes to finish a job – keeps going however long it takes.
- Logical and analytical – technically very able – knowledgeable, good with systems.
- Honest – likes to stick to the rules – strict moral code, doesn't cut corners.
- Thrives on routine and clear expectations. Likes to have a fixed ordered plan. Doesn't get bored with routine or repetition.
- Doesn't waste time chatting, socialising or bothering with 'office politics' – prefers to get on with the job.
- Happy to work independently.
- Loyal. If the person likes the work, he or she is likely to stick with it. Unlikely to be searching for new experiences or fresh challenges.

Less positive qualities of people with AS in the workplace include the following:

- Teamwork skills often poor – not good at fitting in with a group and socialising.

- Communication of own needs poor – not very good at recognising stress, communicating own needs and asking for help.
- When stressed prone to emotional explosions or 'meltdowns'.
- Conflict resolution sometimes poor – can fall out with people due to rather rigid views and intolerances.
- Poor executive skills, poor organisation and planning, poor at juggling multiple tasks, switching attention, prioritising, making decisions.
- Misinterpreting instructions – needs clear unambiguous instructions and sometimes others to check out that message is understood.
- Coping with change poor – needs plenty of warning and preparation for change.
- Management of others can be problematic – due to not recognising the needs of others, lack of flexibility and difficulty resolving conflict.
- Possible unconventional habits and manners may make more vulnerable to teasing.

5 Turning a special interest into a career

People with AS often have all encompassing, strong special interests, in which they have accumulated vast pools of specialist knowledge, skill and expertise. Why not attempt to use that interest to develop a career? Universities are full of people with special interests who are paid to talk about their subjects. Here follows three examples of people who have used their special interest to build a career.

Farook was born in a poor village in Sudan, and both his parents were illiterate. At school he was always top of his class but socially he didn't interact well and was bullied. He was not particularly popular at school because he used to correct the teachers, was opinionated, awkward and poor at sports. He spent most of his childhood reading, especially newspapers, and listening to news bulletins. From a very early age he knew all the members of the political Cabinet and the capital of all the countries in the world and studied Arabic poetry, being able to remember hundreds of lines of poetry quite easily. He eventually went to the university in Khartoum where he studied English language and enjoyed translation work. He came to the UK in 2001 applying for political asylum and eventually obtained a job as a translator and Middle East expert and media analyst. He became so passionate about translating that he spent hours and hours after work doing translation work. He commented: 'Translating is my passion – I would do it for free. I almost can't believe people are paying me to do this.'

Fay who works as a museum curator commented:

> At secondary school people used to think I was rather odd as I hated sport and was not interested in pop music or make-up. I was interested in Sir Francis Drake and the Elizabethans and then slightly later, the Egyptians and the Druids. I studied archaeology at university and eventually became a museum curator. I had to pinch myself the other day when I was cataloguing Roman pottery and I realise I was doing something I really enjoyed and was being paid for it.

Marie is a lawyer who specialises in family law and commented:

> As a 12-year-old I remember going to my local magistrate and Crown Court and sitting in the visitors' gallery being fascinated by the proceedings. The law became something of an obsession to me. I'm now working as a solicitor specialising in family law. I still struggle with the people, and my eye contact is not good, but once a client gets to know me they know I know my business and will do the best for them.

6 Work stress: Social demands

The problem is often not the AS person's ability to do the job, but often comes with the social and interpersonal side of work, communication between the person with AS and their manager and colleagues, sensory issues, coping with overload, changes to routine and coping with stress. One man said: 'It almost feels like I have two jobs simultaneously rather than one. One is doing my work, which I enjoy and am good at; the other is expending huge amounts of energy on maintaining a social interface.' Another lady commented about the general stresses in her job just before Christmas:

> I'm only doing a small clerical job at the university and sometimes think, 'what is the point?'. I've told them I'm not going to the Christmas party, but this week there was a leaving lunch for somebody and my work colleagues laid out all the food on my desk! Then somebody has thought up this idea of having a cocktail competition, where we're all put in teams. I don't want to be involved. I'm there to work.

Tip: Try to strike a balance between assertively saying 'no' to social events and compromising and joining in some events for a limited time. If appropriate disclose reasons to key colleagues.

7 Work stress: Being successful and being promoted – the 'halo effect'

The 'halo effect' is a common scenario within the business world, that is, if a person is good at one particular job, people assume that they will be brilliant with everything, resulting in the person being promoted to being a manager. But managing other people is a completely different skill set from 'doing the job'. Ashley Stanford's book, *Business for 'Aspies'* (2011), is based on her experience of working with her husband Michael, who has an AS diagnosis, and is an exceptionally gifted technically programmer. Together the couple have successfully developed an IT company in the Silicon Valley area of the US. She tells the story of how Michael, earlier in his career, was promoted to manage others because he was such a great programmer and problem solver. His limited time as a manager always ended in disaster because he just wanted to be left alone to write a good code; he had difficulty 'putting himself in others' shoes' and empathising with and understanding the needs of others when they were different from his own. Stanford describes in her book the environment she has had to create for her husband to work at his optimal level. An overriding message of the book is, 'Focus on the positives and the negatives disappear'. However, in this situation the moral is that the brightest and most able person is often not the best manager.

Success also brings rewards that sometimes might be stressful and challenging. In the UK, singer Susan Boyle won a TV talent show, and her records began selling in millions – success changed her life as she became a celebrity. The demands of coping with appearing on TV chat shows, being interviewed by journalists, photographed by the paparazzi and having her private life scrutinised were a very different skill set from singing a song in tune. Susan had undiagnosed Asperger's and didn't cope.

Rebecca, a research scientist at a university, was investigating climate change and cloud formations and made a research breakthrough. She had an article published in the prestigious journal *Nature* – with her photograph on the front cover. She commented:

> Overnight I became something of a celebrity, having my photograph in the newspaper, being interviewed on television and by the press and being invited to champagne receptions at various universities. I found these social functions extremely stressful as I was happiest on my own, sitting at my desk, quietly analysing the data. I became increasingly anxious and stressed until I had a 'nervous breakdown' and made a suicide attempt. I was referred to a Community Mental Health Team, who mistakenly diagnosed borderline personality disorder. After over a year of medication and not very helpful psychological therapy, I was diagnosed as having Asperger's syndrome. It was like someone had turned the lights on.

Tip: Recognise your strengths and weaknesses. Good technicians might not make good managers. Think about the skills required to be a good manager and decide whether you have those skills. Talk it over with somebody who will give you good feedback.

8 Work stress: Sudden unexpected change

People with AS thrive on routine, sameness, predictability and knowing what is coming next. Variety is not the spice of life, and the emotion of surprises is often the equivalent of terror. People often say they are physically ill preparing for change. Jim had worked for the post office for 20 years sorting the mail and his story is relevant.

> I'd studied history at university, but enjoyed the sorting job because it gave me an income, a regular rhythm and routine and I could listen to my audio tapes on the history of the First and Second World War while I worked. I had my own sorting frame with different compartments for different postcodes and areas and was the quickest sorters of mail in the south east of England. One Monday morning I came in and my sorting frame had been moved. A new management team decided that they wanted to implement some changes and decided to move me to a work on a different area and take on more responsibility. I was absolutely furious and had a real 'meltdown' with the new manager, pinning him against a wall. I was suspended, had a breakdown, resulting in nine months off work. I saw a psychiatrist for depression, and then got a referral to a psychologist who diagnosed Asperger's syndrome. I did manage to successfully return to work but not before all managers within the sorting office were given autism awareness training.

Tip: Alert managers that sudden change is particularly stressful and it needs to be gradual. Talk it through with a friend or colleague, identifying the difficulties, ways of coping and benefits.

9 Work stress: Failing to 'read between the lines' – misinterpreting communication

Reading between the lines, or interpreting complex information that might be ambiguous, is sometimes a problem. Alan had worked for the Ministry of Defence on an army base for 15 years as a warehouseman and delivery driver. He was conscientious and really enjoyed his job, although he wasn't very sociable and had a number of 'run-ins' and fallouts with people and was known as being 'a little odd or eccentric'. He usually arrived at work between 07.40 and 08.00 every morning and often worked over his allotted hours or through his lunch break so that he got the job done. A number of influential friendly colleagues had always said, 'It doesn't matter exactly what time you get in as long as the job is done'. The Ministry of defence then launched an initiative called 'Flexible Working Hours Policy', which came in a four-page document, with complicated language, multiple clauses and small print. Computerised time sheets were also introduced. Alan signed the document, without fully understanding it, thinking that he was agreeing to carry on working 'flexibly'. A senior manager had even commented, 'just carry on with the flexi'. However, although the policy document was entitled 'Flexible Working Hours', what it really meant was the opposite. Employees were given a choice of a number of shifts and then had to stick to those shifts. Alan had signed the form for the shift that expected employees to arrive at 07.30 and work until 04.00. But because the document was entitled 'Flexible Working Hours Policy', Alan took the meaning literally and carried on as previously getting in at between 07.30 and 07.50 and working after 04.00 to complete a job if it was required. Alan had moved from one department to another and didn't have a settled line manager and nobody had spelt out to him what he needed to do and what he was doing was wrong. Because he was rather isolated and didn't mix with his co-workers at breaks and lunchtime, he didn't get the feedback and information that might have occurred in casual chit-chat. Unfortunately, Alan was disciplined and was suspended. At the time Alan didn't have a diagnosis of AS and received one only a year later after he had collapsed into depression.

Tip: Seek help in understanding complex ambiguous legal communication from a trustworthy person. Check out the meaning. Ask, 'Have I missed something here?'

10 Work stress: Being too blunt and upsetting others

People with AS often say what they think in a very direct, blunt manner, without considering the emotional impact on the listener. This can often create problems in the workplace. Ceara was a senior nurse, married with children, who had worked in the paediatric intensive care unit of a large teaching hospital for 20 years with undiagnosed AS. She commented:

> I've always been really good with the technical stuff, medical information, and medications – better than most of the doctors. I don't get attached to patients and just get on with it. I'm a bit robotic in my dealings with patients and their relatives, but I have recently learned to say, 'I'm sorry' to a relative if a baby dies. My communication difficulties have always been brought up in appraisals. I recently got suspended from work for apparently bullying another member of staff, but I wasn't bullying her, I was just telling her what she had done wrong, so she wouldn't make the same mistake next time. I suppose I might have been a bit blunt or outspoken and didn't really take into account that she was upset after the little baby had died. After I got the diagnosis and went back to work I told my colleagues and asked them for more direct feedback, saying, 'tell me if I'm being too blunt or if I've upset you. I can't tell and there is no intention.'

Tip: Ask for feedback from a trusted colleague. Tell people your judgement is suspect and you might need help. Give people permission saying, 'tell me if I'm being a bit direct' or too blunt.

11 Work stress: Sensory overload

Work environments can pose all kinds of stresses in terms of assaulting our senses, particularly with noise, light and smell. Flickering neon lights, noisy open plan offices, groups of people chatting, people with strong scent or aftershave are recognised problems. If stress levels are already high, such additions can easily tip people over the edge. Eden worked in an office and made the following comments:

> They moved some other people into the open plan office and one had a really noisy computer, which really affected my concentration. We called IT in and they found that it was vibrating on the desk, so we put padding underneath. Another woman was constantly jiggling her feet behind me and I could feel the vibrations on the floor – it drives me mad! Then they interviewed a lady for a job who smelt of really strong perfume – a melange of odours. I felt like saying please don't employ that person. It's the social side and sensory side of the job which make me feel stressed. The job itself is a doddle.

Tip: Tell your manager and try to create the optimal environment to work in. See the chapter on managing sensory sensitivities (chapter 7).

12 Work stress: Overload and 'meltdowns'

Overwhelming sensory input from lights, noise and smells combined with multiple mental and social demands often leads to overload, ensuing internal panic and 'meltdowns'. Often it is a build-up of little things over the course of a day and then a final straw that leads to a loss of internal stability and a downwards spiral. People with AS often don't have a very good gauge to filter how much stress is piling up, and end up crashing after the stress becomes too much. It is crucial that we recognise overload and its consequences. Meltdowns are an example of the fight-or-flight response – either an angry outburst, or running away or playing dead and being passive. People end up getting angry or anxious and saying or doing things they regret, losing relationships and jobs.

Richard commented:

> I lost my previous job because I had a meltdown – I got angry with a colleague. My manager at the time said it was the last straw even though I was doing the job better than anyone else. In my present job I have 'come out' and told my manager I have Asperger's and can occasionally lose it and become an inarticulate spluttering angry person. What I said is 'please don't take it personally – it's not personal'. It's the situation that makes me so frustrated that my 'inner switch' is flipped – I'm a bit like Jekyll and Hyde – I can't escape from the monster in me. Usually I need to retire to a quiet place where I can be alone for a while so I can decompress and wait for the inner switch to flip back to the calm mode.

Carol commented:

Sometimes I have to just get out – but there is nowhere private as my office is all open plan and the building I work in just has glass offices. I either go for a walk in my heavy coat with a big hood or I go to my car in the underground car park. I keep a sleeping bag and can curl up on the back seat pulling the bag over my head for 10 minutes. Then I feel recharged and better able to cope.

Tip: Try to anticipate stress build-up and leave the situation, retreating to a calm environment. Tell people. Apologise afterwards. See the section on coping with meltdowns. (chapter 8, p155)

13 Work stress: Getting through the job interview

For most jobs there is an interview process which can be problematic for people with AS. One man said:

> I'm bad at interviews because I can't explain myself or answer questions on the spot – I need time. I find it difficult to understand the nuance

> of the questions when the questions have several meanings. I think my autism affects my ability to give a good first impression at interview – I come across as awkward. In fact my last boss said, 'I really wasn't sure about you at the interview but you've turned out really well'. I also think that a major problem these days is that the pendulum has swung too far in the direction of 'must be a good team player'.

A good idea is to practice beforehand, maybe role playing with a trusted person firing questions at the applicant. It is also sensible for the person being interviewed to make a list of behaviour they should and shouldn't do. Examples might be: make appropriate greeting, make good eye contact, don't bite nails. Philip Wylie (2015) reports that he has had some success with the unusual strategy of when applying for a job, to volunteer his services free of charge for a few days before the interview. In that way employers became more aware of his skills and abilities to compensate for his awkward performance at the interview.

Tip: Some coaching and preparation for interview might be a good idea. Also, some soft disclosure, where there is an acknowledgement that there is a difference between being good at an interview and doing the job itself might help.

14 Managing eye contact and other non-verbal behaviours

To survive in the work arena, there is a need to try to improve or at least conceal poor eye contact. The eyes are a powerful communication tool and, without intending, can cause people with AS serious problems at work. Because of poor eye contact, they might be accused of being 'shifty'; conversely, staring eye contact might lead to claims of sexual harassment. An assertive step for people with AS is to tell colleagues at work that they have difficulties with eye contact and reading people's facial expression, by saying something like:

> I'm sorry but I do not read faces as well as most people do. Could you explain what you mean in words rather than showing me via your face? Alternatively, 'I'm sorry if my eye contact is poor but I have a sensory integration disorder and find it difficult to look at someone and listen to them at the same time. I am listening to every word you say even though I'm not looking'.

If eye contact is a major personal problem, it might be best to focus on jobs that have less face time or are often more flexible where you either work on your own, or from home or from a remote office.

Tips for managing poor eye contact

- *Look near their eyes*, maybe at their forehead or upper lip rather than directly in the other person's eyes.
- *Glance away often*, but when the other person looks away take the opportunity to look at their face.
- *Allow your eyes to glaze over* – allow your eyes to relax; think of something enjoyable.

15 Different thinking styles for different jobs

Temple Grandin in her book *The Autistic Brain* (2014), which was co-edited with Richard Panek, makes some interesting suggestions about how there are different types of autistic brains which determine the person's particular skill and therefore the type of job that they might be best at. She had previously written a bestselling book entitled *Thinking in Pictures*, which describes how she had visualised humane livestock-handling facilities. She points out that she was the visual thinker and thought of the concepts such as the layout of the plant – the slaughter house, the packaging floor and so on, but that it was the 'pattern thinker', the qualified engineer, who calculated the roof trusses, the spacing and the concrete specifications. Grandin initially made the assumption that the majority of autistic people think in pictures like her, until confronted by a member of her audience at a presentation who disagreed. Grandin now suggests that there are three systems of thinking: visual or picture thinkers, verbal thinkers and a new category called pattern thinkers. Since then she has gone on to identify different types of jobs that fit those thinking styles.

First comes *picture thinking*, where the brain has an ability to visualise an object or picture and, in Grandin's case, allowed her to visualise how frightening it was for a cow to be herded into a channel with sharp turns, and to imagine a more rounded humane system. She could imagine, almost as a film in her head or her imagination, what she wanted and then needed to find someone to create it for her in reality. The picture thinker might be good at art or designing jewellery, cooking or woodwork. The second category is the *pattern thinkers,* where the person can visualise a pattern or structure, in the sense that they imagine the ways the parts of an object fit together where there is an element of organisation. The pattern thinker loves Lego and other construction toys and has an eye for detail. Pattern thinkers are good at maths, music and engineering, understanding the form behind the function; they can fix computers, build bridges and build the livestock systems that Temple Grandin visualised. The third category is the *word fact thinker*, where the person thinks in words and facts and often has a good memory, for statistics, dates or scientific bits of information. They can often remember words, sometimes even the whole script of a film, important statistics, scientific bits of information or dates and numbers. Word fact thinkers see the details, dot the *I*s and cross the *T*s. They are good at record keeping, organising data bases, filing, working in a bank.

Jobs for picture thinkers	Jobs for word fact thinkers
• Architect	• Translator
• Photographer	• Librarian
• Graphic artist	• Copy editor/proofreader
• Web designer	• Accountant
• Computer troubleshooter	• Book and record keeper
• Landscape gardener	• Technical writer
• Satellite map analyst	• Translator
• Plumber	• Data analyst
• Engineer	• Speech therapist
• Computer animator	• Information officer
• Technician	• Writer
• Cartographer	• University lecturer/researcher
• Artist	
Jobs for pattern thinkers	**Jobs with structure and limited face time**
• Computer programmer	• Cleaner
• Engineer	• Gardener
• Physicist	• Driver – coach/taxi/bus
• Music composer	• Assembly line worker
• Statistician	• Craftsman
• Chemist	• Horticulturalist
• Scientific researcher	• Safety/security officer
• Actuary	• Postman
• Mathematical/financial analyst	• Animal trainer
• Music or maths teacher	• Delivery person
• Electrician	
• Movement/dance notary	

Different thinkers complement each other. Grandin says that she co-authored the book *The Autistic Brain* with a man called Richard Panek and commented how well they worked as a team. She was a picture thinker and visualised the main ideas and the overall picture, and he picked out the patterns and structured and organised the book. She gives the example regarding the popular Apple iPod and iPhone saying that Steve Jobs, the founder of Apple, was the man who had the vision (picture thinker); he knew what he wanted and how beautiful he wanted it to look like. But, he needed engineers (pattern thinkers), to put his ideas into practice.

16 Tips for managing someone with Asperger's syndrome

Here are a number of simple tips that might be helpful for managers working with individuals with AS.

- **Explain tasks clearly**: Try to be clear and specific, avoiding the abstract vague and hypothetical and possibly supplement spoken instructions with written instructions.
- **One task at a time:** It's probably best to deal with one task at a time rather than giving them multiple tasks at the same time. Remember people with AS are likely to be very good at focusing on one task but poor at multitasking or shifting focus.
- **Avoid ambiguous language**: Try to avoid ambiguous open-ended questions. For example, 'Tell me about yourself' is very vague and they may not be able to judge what information to give.
- **Be aware that people with AS may interpret language literally**: Asking 'How did you find your last job?' may result in 'I looked at the map' or 'I saw an advert in the paper'.
- **Check it out:** Ask if they have understood and give regular feedback about their performance. If they are talking too much let them know and give feedback, as they may find it hard to judge.
- **Communication difficulties are unintentional:** People with AS often say the 'wrong' thing and can be socially awkward and blunt. But remember this is probably unintentional. Remind other colleagues where appropriate.

- **Socialising difficulties:** People with AS have difficulty socialising, networking and making friends. Allowances need to be made.
- **Try to find causes of their anxiety:** People with AS might not be fully aware of what is stressing them – try to find out in a one-to-one session.
- **Don't take it personally:** AS people can be blunt, brutally honest, fail to take into account the feelings of others and have 'meltdowns'. Try not to take it personally as there is probably no malice or forethought.
- **Be aware of change:** People with AS like routine and predictability and might even say, 'I love this job because every day is the same'. This can be an advantage, but if change is needed, gradually prepare them for it.
- **Be aware of sensory issues – prepare the environment:** People with AS may be particularly sensitive to noise, light, smells, touch or temperature and may not be very good at filtering things out and be easily 'overloaded'. A seat by the window might help.

17 Tips for people with Asperger's syndrome to cope with work

- **Make time for yourself:** When presented with somebody asking for a decision and you are not ready, practice the pre-scripted response of saying, 'Can I get back to you later in the day?'. Give yourself time to consider a reasonable response.
- **Try to keep brain space:** Keep brain space and self-protect against overload by focusing on one thing at a time. Ignore the rest. If you are a hyperfocuser, your brain doesn't want to be seeing too many things to do at once.
- **Control your working environment:** Try wearing headphones when working to block out distraction noise, have your favourite

soundtrack on your headphones that can help you calm down, dim the lights on your desk, have a drawer full of fidget toys, things you can play with like a Rubik's cube.

- **Learn to say 'no' and prioritise:** This is a key assertiveness skill in any walk of life. We all have only a limited capacity and it is important to work out what to prioritise and what to say 'no' to. This is easier said than done and is an area where you might have to ask for help from a job coach, manager or friend.
- **Asking for help:** This is often a good idea as it shows you are engaged in team work. Tell people you might not always be able to interpret their facial expression or moods and might need a few extra clues.
- **Have somewhere to escape to:** One useful strategy is to find a safe place to escape to when things become too overwhelming.

Chapter Fourteen

After diagnosis: Reactions, disclosure and advice

1 People's reaction to the diagnosis of Asperger's syndrome

People's reactions to diagnosis vary, but a majority experience it positively; for some it is a life-changing event, a shift in perspective, an epiphanic moment. For some it is a nomadic journey looking for the answer to questions, consulting numerous professionals and then finally finding the answers to many things that have puzzled or confused. One man said. 'It was the best news I ever had in my life ... I feel like nothing has changed but everything is different. Everything all of a sudden makes sense. The ugly duck is now a swan' (Santomauro, p26). Other people have made similar comments about the life-changing nature of getting a diagnosis.

- 'It was like somebody turning the lights on. Before my diagnosis I was stumbling around in the dark always bumping into the furniture.'
- 'It was like being in court and getting a not guilty verdict.'
- 'I found the key to my life ... The diagnosis set me free to be who I really am.'

My colleague Louise Ackers and I carried out a follow-up research study (2015) of 74 people who had received a diagnosis in the previous three months. One of the questions we posed in our study was, 'How did getting a diagnosis make you feel?'. The written responses were divided into six main themes which were as follows: (1) *Relief* – 73 per cent reported being relieved or pleased, stating, 'I was relieved to have it confirmed'; 'relief that it's not caused by my inadequacy' or 'not to be labelled a 'weirdo'. (2) *Positive feelings linked to the sense of self*: 'I feel more empowered'; 'makes me feel glad, stronger, independent'; 'I feel validated'; 'I feel more understood'. One person described an almost euphoric experience: 'I was so happy I could not sleep that night. I was 'high' for about two weeks ... the only thing I could compare it with was falling in love'. (3) *Mixed feelings:* 'Relieved but daunted ... angry and sad that it wasn't picked up earlier'. 'Initially I felt relieved, but at times it feels like confirmation that I am unlikely ever to be normal'. The process of being diagnosed seemed to trigger reflection about past experiences, and some participants described being upset or angry that the diagnosis had not been previously recognised. They stated: 'I was upset, because I thought back to many instances in my life and how different and better they would have been if I had been diagnosed earlier in life'; '[I am] very sad to think my life would be far better today if I had known earlier'. (4) *Negative feelings* – this occurred particularly among younger people: 'shocked because I didn't think I had it' and 'angry that if it's 1 in a 100, why does it have to be me? I'm annoyed' and 'It's a bit depressing – confirmation that I will never feel "normal" or will not "get better".' (5) *No clear feelings*: approximately 10 per cent described having no immediate emotional reaction to the diagnosis, or not being able to describe or label any emotion. Their comments were: 'It has had no effect – I feel no different'; 'I am not bothered'; 'I don't know how I feel about it'; 'I will have to go away and assimilate it – it takes me a while to work through how I feel'. However, for many in this group, getting a diagnosis had more meaning and impact for family members, friends and clinicians, who now had an explanation for the diagnosed person's behaviour. (6) *Diagnostic disappointment*: There is a small group of people who come along hoping for a diagnosis, but leave disappointed that they do not get the full diagnosis, but could be described as having traits, residual Asperger's or social communication difficulties. One person summarised: 'I was hoping that the assessment would give me clear answers but it didn't. I'm disappointed and feel that I'm stuck in limbo.'

A dilemma for the assessor is what name or label to give to the person in the 'subclinical threshold group'. The new DSM-5 has 'Social and Communication Disorder' as a separate diagnosis and ICD-10 has 'atypical autism', but terms such as 'mild Asperger's',

'Asperger's residual', 'Autistic traits', 'broader autistic phenotype', 'autistic like personality', or 'on the autistic spectrum' could be used. A further dilemma for the diagnosing clinician is how broad or narrow to interpret the medical classification categories, when dealing with a condition on a dimensional scale.

2 What effect does getting a diagnosis have on people's lives?

When asked the question, 'What is the main effect of the assessment on your life?', the overwhelming response, expressed by 83 per cent of respondents, was the theme that it (1) *provided understanding and explanation*: 'It puts the pieces together in my mind ... helps because it explains so much ... I reflected on my past.' Many participants made comments indicating that the diagnosis allowed them to understand themselves better: 'It allows me to understand ... the root of the problem'; 'it answered 50 years' worth of questions'. Understanding could be retrospective and prompted reflection: 'When I look back on my life in the light of the diagnosis, things make more sense'; 'I have spent time retracing awkward moments'; 'Now I know why I have struggled with social situations all these years'. (2) *It made me feel better about myself*: Participants reported that their sense of worth had improved following diagnosis. For some, the diagnosis provided a greater level of self-acceptance: 'In a very real way, the diagnosis has validated my life and made me able to accept that I am not just a failure with a large IQ.' For many participants, the diagnosis had helped them to reattribute blame from self to the diagnosis: 'I am more content with myself because I know it's not my fault'; 'I have permission to accept that I find some things hard'. Interestingly, in many cases, getting a diagnosis prompted people to act with greater confidence and self-compassion: 'It helped me gain confidence in who I am'; 'Having a diagnosis means I don't have to spend my time trying to fix myself'; 'I can tell my nice but naive psychological therapist that there are things about myself that I can't change. My task is then to accept how I am. It's the way my brain is wired.' For some, feeling better about themselves was linked to improvement in mental health: 'Although I still feel like a misfit, I feel better about myself – my mental health has stabilised.' (3) *Tangible gains and support*: Some described the diagnosis as positively 'opening the way' for tangible gains including study support, financial benefits, AS-related specialist support and AS-friendly working practices. 'It helped me get study support at university'; 'It opened the way for tangible gains ... benefits'; 'Improved my job prospect ... work must now make reasonable allowances'. (4) *Relationships effected both positively and negatively*: One man commented, 'Work understands me more now'; some said, 'My family understands me more now'. One woman commented on how it had improved her marriage: 'My husband said it doesn't change anything, "I love you for who you are, not a label". But now I can explain to him why I can't do certain things or need the volume turned down. It's brought a positive understanding of each other.' However, although the majority of social responses were positive, there were some negatives too: 'My boyfriend treats me differently now. I'm more aware of being scrutinised.' There was also an awareness of other people's expectations changing: 'It limits the expectations of others, who watch me more closely, or assume I'll never be able to do things at work or home that I can do.'

3 Disclosure

A major issue for everybody who gets a late-in-life diagnosis is disclosure. There are two issues here: first, whether to disclose and, second, how much, when, to whom and why. There is no absolute right or wrong and some people tell everybody, some tell nobody. In general, it is better to be honest, but there are many factors to consider, and it is a complex personal decision. Philip Wylie (2015) sensibly suggests that it is important to become self-aware, having some understanding of the condition, to know your strengths and weaknesses, before disclosing to others. If people with AS have accepted it themselves and understand it, they are in a better position to explain to others clearly. It might be a good idea to devise a list of traits and behaviours that can be attributed to AS. For example, saying, 'I'm easily agitated in crowds or if people frown I can't tell if they are sad, angry or lonely etc'. He points out that it is exhausting not being true to oneself and can sometimes lead to mental health difficulties.

Liane Holliday Willey (2015) suggests that disclosure has to be dealt with by two groups: those who need to know and those who might not need to know. The need to know group includes people in a position of authority, such as employers, teachers, doctors, people with whom those with AS have a strong trustworthy relationship with and individuals to whom they might turn to for advice and support. The group that might not need to know includes tradespersons, people who have occasional contact, distant relatives, strangers or friends with whom people with AS have lost contact.

It is important to be prepared if disclosing for the following reactions. One possibility is that elderly parents might be too set in their ways, too conservative in their thinking and might feel slightly guilty that they didn't pick it up before, to embrace the truth warmly. One typical reaction came from Steven, aged 40, who commented, 'My dad doesn't think it exists'. A further possible reaction is that because AS is so subtle to the casual observer, people's reactions might be: 'There's nothing wrong; it's just the latest psychobabble, or a way of making excuses for yourself.' With friends and acquaintances it is important to be discerning, as there is a lot of misinformation, and the worst case scenario is that people might confuse the AS diagnosis with a mental illness. Unfortunately, some people might want to exclude the person disclosing from their social group. With partners in a long-term relationship, he suggests, that open disclosure may be beneficial and create a certain freedom, but warns 'The truth may set you free but it doesn't necessarily set everybody else free'.

There are advantages and disadvantages to disclosure. The advantages are: (1) It might make the person feel safer, if the telling brings people closer into their support corner. (2) It might help the person relax, reduce the pressure that concealment brings, more able to be their real self, no longer needing to pretend. (3) It helps to educate others and increases the proportion of people that understand and know about the condition. When a person with AS does 'come out' they are not only doing it for themselves, but they also become part of a broader 'neurodiversity movement' that will pave the way for other autistic people to have a smoother ride. (4) If the person is in a long-term intimate relationship it may be wise to tell in order to improve intimacy. (5) It might be important to tell, to obtain support at college, financial benefits or treatment for mental health issues. (6) At work it might be necessary to change the environment to accommodate sensory issues. (7) It might be a last resort, a risk worth taking, when the person can't bear faking it any more.

The negatives of disclosure are: (1) It might alter the listener's perception of the person and what they are capable of doing, increasing reservations and doubts about the person's abilities. (2) It might create pity or worry that the person is not up to the task in hand. (3) It might increase the risk of being further ostracised, or being seen as 'damaged goods'. (4) The listener may not have any knowledge about the diagnosis or have a false understanding.

There is something called 'soft disclosure' or disclosure of certain difficulties rather than 'hard disclosure' of a specific diagnosis. One man commented to a co-worker about his reluctance to go to a social event, 'I'm good at complex tasks but an idiot at simple things like small talk'. Soft disclosure invites allowances and adjustments by confessing shortcomings but avoids the sometimes stigmatising disability label. A 'drip effect' where information is given gradually, on a need-to-know basis, can also be advantageous. At work it also might be best to disclose to a trusted colleague first and see how it goes from there. Derek commented: 'I choose not to fully disclose because of the inevitability of being treated like a "case". Instead I am slowly opening up about my autistic traits without giving them a label so that people can treat me as a person who is overfocused and has quirky ways rather than someone who is autistic.' Liane Holliday Willey suggests keeping it short and simple with people who you will only have brief contact with. She explains that she frequently says things like, 'Would you do me a favour? I have a specific learning difficulty that makes it hard for me to understand jargon and abstract concepts. Could you please explain it in a concrete and simple way so I will be more likely to really understand you? I'm not dense I just have a problem with language and non-verbal communication.'

Coming out, or disclosing at work, can be part of a long process and it might be better to come out elsewhere first. In one survey, about a third of people said that they have fully disclosed at work, one-third disclosed to one or two close colleagues and a third avoided disclosure completely. AS is recognised as a 'hidden disability' by law, and the Equality Act (2010) offers some protection in the workplace where employees are legally bound to make 'reasonable adjustments'. If a person is applying for a job and there is competition for the vacancy, mentioning a diagnosis, which might be unknown to the employer, on an application form, might lead to the person being rejected. Tony Attwood suggests, one possibility worth considering, is to write a brief one-page description of AS – a personalised statement.

4 Advice for others after diagnosis

At the end of this book, I would like to give the final word to the people this book is about, namely, the people who have received a diagnosis late in life. I asked a number of my clients: 'What advice would you give to others who might be in the same position and had recently received a diagnosis?'. Here are some replies that are mixed with some comments from the literature.

Gain understanding and self-knowledge

- 'Read about it, especially the personal accounts – educate yourself. But bear in mind people are different. I have found reading helps with self-understanding and self-knowledge and identifying what my needs are. Tony Attwood's book is still incredibly useful.'
- 'Go online – join forums. There is an excellent Facebook page/internet site called "The Curly Haired Project". It is able to put things into words which really help me explain to others. The internet is like a classroom full of research and people's stories.'
- 'I joined Wrong Planet, an online autism forum, and found the people were very welcoming.'
- 'I joined Autism Berkshire and attended a workshop.'
- 'I attended a post-diagnostic support and education group – Being Me – which was helpful in understanding Asperger's, but also in meeting others with similar issues.'
- 'I'm beginning to understand my own needs better. For example, I need time alone and I've made a rule that I will limit any socialising to a maximum of two hours. My advice is, "Recognise your own needs and assertively try to get them met".'
- 'I researched online ways that I could change my lifestyle in order to reduce my stress and anxiety and to gain a better understanding of why I felt and behave the way I do. For example, I found out a great deal about aphantasia and alexithymia.'
- 'Go to training seminars.'

Don't forget your strengths

- 'Remind yourself of your autistic strengths. Think of all the successful famous people who have been autistic – brilliant minds that have changed the world. Write down a list of all your strengths – things you can do that others can't.'
- 'Keep a journal to record insights and transformational experiences or write a blog – I find writing therapeutic and it helps me to piece things together.'
- 'Turn hobbies and special interests – your strengths – into therapeutic activities and career opportunities.'
- 'Celebrate your difference. AS is a design feature – it's good. We are not broken; we are wonderfully unique thinkers. The world needs us to keep you honest.'
- Don't get too caught up in the label – I am still 'me' with lots of strengths.

Seek support

- 'Immerse yourself into some kind of autistic community, whether it is a group, an online forum or watching videos of people sharing their experience. Being with people or somebody with the same condition is comforting, knowing you are not alone. I find myself saying, "That's how it is for me".'
- 'I talked to close friends and family about the diagnosis and what it meant for my relationships with them. Support from these people was vital and continues to be so.'
- "I need support in the form of somebody just giving me the occasional prompt, or reminder of how to think and deal with situations.'
- 'I would suggest find a support group. The six-week post-diagnostic group was helpful.'
- 'I've got a friend who has agreed to be my "check out person". I can ring her if I'm unsure or confused about something.'

- 'At university, my counsellor put me in touch with a friendship group for people with Asperger's.
- 'It's helpful to find a professional clinician who will be supportive.'
- 'I like the idea of having a mentor, somebody with AS who would be positive and would be a guide for the journey I am now on.'
- 'I think something needs to be in place for the partner of the person receiving the diagnosis as this revelation can hit both parties equally hard. My partner was negative and concluded that I was damaged goods. What I could have done with is meeting a positive person who could have calmed my partner and inspired me.'
- 'Analyse your family history to identify the genetic path of autism. Finding out there are relatives who might have had the condition made me somehow feel better and more forgiving of myself.'

Use practical strategies

- 'I carry a card (autism alert card) just in case I find myself in a challenging situation and either have a meltdown or shutdown. I've never had to use it but the fact that it's there is comforting.'
- 'I now know why a structured day makes me feel calmer, so every day I have a plan and a list. I also have taught myself to accept that things don't go according to plan and that is not the end of the world. It's normal!'
- 'Connect more with nature and its healing powers. Most autistic people are peaceful people who enjoy nature and animals.'
- 'Live in a foreign country or marry a person from a different culture. This helps because people from a different culture are less aware and less concerned by our differences.'
- 'I shop online and get home delivery, which makes life so much easier.'
- 'I reviewed my employment and took steps to find work that was low stress with an environment that suited my sensory needs.'

- 'I don't communicate with people when I'm angry. I will delay sending that email for 24 hours, then moderate it.'
- 'I carry a small notebook and Post-it stickers to help with my organisational problems.'
- Be kind to yourself
- 'Find something that is relaxing – my most effective way is to perform my special interest which is cycling. I can think on a bike. Meditation and mindfulness have been useful also.'
- 'Don't expect everybody to understand and believe you. Be aware that people don't understand autism, even professionals.'
- 'Beware of the peaks and troughs of mood. Sometimes I think I am getting somewhere and then feel that I'm at the bottom of the learning curve again.'
- 'I know I need a quiet, serene, relaxing place to live – somewhere to unwind. I moved out of a flat where there were noisy neighbours and traffic.'
- 'It's OK to say you need help. It took me a long time to master this!'
- 'I use humour and gently make fun of my idiosyncrasies before anybody else does.'
- 'I found it helpful to reflect on my life up to the point of diagnosis and how I dealt with things. Everything made more sense. I felt that many things that I had been blaming myself for really weren't my fault. I have decided to give myself a break, stop beating myself up and be kinder to myself.'
- 'Everything is a balancing act. I recognise that I have to get a balance between having one foot in the neurotypical world and having one foot in the Aspie world and being myself. I don't think that the two extremes of either being an outright militant "Aspie", walking around not compromising, or hiding away and feeling bad about yourself are helpful. I would suggest the midpoint, which is to be yourself enough to stay sane, but to compromise with the neurotypical world enough to get by – to be bicultural.'

- 'Love and accept your own individuality and things will fall into place. Don't deny you have Asperger's as it only makes the world a harder place to live in.
- "On any given day, I can be just like everyone else seems to be. Until I remember that I do not have to be. The me that I am has finally made friends with the differences I no longer try to hide"' (Liane Holliday Willey, 2015, p112).

Appendix 1

'Being Me' Group: Handouts for a six-week post-diagnostic course

This section consists of a number of handouts that form the basis of a six-week post-diagnostic session, which we entitled, 'Being Me'. It follows NAS self-development resource and DVD of the same name. We use their 'Being Me' DVD to complement the handouts.

The objectives of the groups or courses are for people to (1) meet others in a similar position; (2) learn and understand more about AS; and (3) learn and share coping strategies with others.

Each session usually lasts for two hours with a short break in the middle. The ideal number in a group ranges from five to eight. Each session would normally have two items for discussion and two or three handouts to work through. Most people are very anxious to start off with but by the end of the course are more relaxed exchanging telephone numbers and email addresses.

Our experience is that people like structure in the group and the emphasis on practical suggestions for help. Having handouts, and playing video clips, with specific issues to discuss and questions to answer is beneficial. One tip I have learned, having run seven or eight of these groups, is to ask specific questions, such as, 'Identify one thing you like or agree with and one thing you disagree with or dislike about the video clip', rather than vague open-ended questions, such as, 'What do you think?'. I have been corrected many times for my vagueness!

1 Autism quiz and definitions

Exercise 1: Autism quiz. Read each statement in the following section and state whether it is true or false. Discuss.

Autism is ...		True	False
1	caused by stress		
2	associated with different wiring/connectivity in the brain		
3	more common in boys than girls		
4	the result of unaffectionate parents		
5	associated with repetitive behaviour		
6	a condition that one in a hundred people have		
7	six times more likely to occur if the father is over 40		
8	sometimes associated with genius		
9	something you are born with		
10	a mental health issue		

Answers on the final page of the book.

Exercise 2: Which definition do you prefer? Read each definition for AS and decide which one you think is the best and the worst. Discuss.

(a) AS involves difficulties in social communication and usually strong, narrow interests, repetitive behaviour and sensory sensitivities.

(b) 'Autism' comes from the Greek word '*autos*', meaning 'self'. The condition implies a lack of understanding of others – or difficulty 'putting yourself in somebody else's shoes', or seeing the world from the perspective of another.

(c) 'The autistic brain is highly wired in the areas involved with attention to detail, memory and systematizing – like an eight-lane motorway. But, in areas concerned with the social and emotional world, the connections are poorly wired – like a country lane'.

2 Being on the autism spectrum: Language and labels – your view

Somebody once said, 'If you haven't got a word for it, it doesn't exist'. One of the issues with AS is which words or diagnostic labels to use.

Exercise 1: Which name or diagnostic label do you prefer when referring to yourself? Discuss.

Rank on a 5-point scale: 1 = strongly dislike; 2 = dislike; 3 = neither like nor dislike; 4 = like; 5 = strongly like.

Autistic person		Person with autism	
On the autistic spectrum		Asperger's syndrome	
Autistic spectrum disorder		Autistic spectrum condition	
Aspie		ASD	

Exercise 2: What factors led to you seeking a diagnosis?

....

....

Exercise 3: How would you describe your condition to somebody else if asked?

....

....

Exercise 4: What would you like to learn about being on the autism spectrum?

....

....

....

3 Feelings about getting a diagnosis

The majority of people who seek a diagnosis later in life have mixed feelings but often feel a sense of relief.

Exercise 1: How did you feel about getting a diagnosis? (Tick the relevant boxes)

1 Relieved	☐	5 Confused	☐	9 Depressed	☐
2 Angry	☐	6 Shocked	☐	10 Upset	☐
3 Elated	☐	7 Anxious	☐	11 Alone	☐
4 Nothing	☐	8 Frustrated	☐	12 Surprised	☐

Please list any other feelings you had.

....

....

Exercise 2: Write a sentence that best describes your emotional reaction to getting a diagnosis.

....

....

....

Exercise 3: What aspect of your life is affected the most by getting a diagnosis?..

....

....

Exercise 4: Do you agree with this statement? Discuss.

'People with autism are just different, not disabled. We don't want a cure, treatment or sympathy, just acceptance.'

....

....

4 How does being on the autism spectrum affect me?

Everybody with AS is affected differently. It is important to understand your own profile of strengths and weaknesses.

Exercise 1: Read the following statements and tick the boxes next to the statements that best describe you – tick as many boxes as appropriate. Discuss.

1 I have special interests that I can be rather obsessive about. ☐

2 I can be very blunt and upset other people without meaning to. ☐

3 I find it difficult to tell if someone listening to me is getting bored. ☐

4 When I read a story I find it difficult to work out the characters' intentions. ☐

5 I don't like change and prefer a predictable routine. ☐

6 I find social situations challenging and often want to be on my own. ☐

7 I find it hard to tell when other people are joking or being sarcastic. ☐

8 I'm not very good at small talk. ☐

9 I am very sensitive to touch or certain textures or smells or particular noises. ☐

10 I often find it hard to know what other people are feeling and thinking. ☐

11 I usually concentrate more on the details rather the whole picture. ☐

12 If there is an interruption, I find it difficult to switch back to what I was doing. ☐

13 I find it difficult to 'read between the lines' when someone is talking to me. ☐

14 I am not very good at noticing how I am feeling. ☐

Exercise 2: Add one more statement about yourself. This could either be something you find hard, or something that makes you feel different from others.

....

....

5 Sensory sensitivities

Many people with AS have sensory sensitivities, where their senses are either heightened or lessened or are not integrated.

Exercise: Fill out the table to work out what your sensory sensitivities are (if you have any) and how you could cope with them. Discuss.

Sense	Sensitivity *(eg 'I don't like the uncomfortable feel of rough, scratching fabric')*	Coping strategy *(eg 'I line my trousers, cut out labels in clothes and avoid wool products')*
Sound	....	....
Taste	....	....
Touch	....	....
Vision	....	....
Smell	....	....
Coordination and balance	....	....
Any other	....	....

6 Positive aspects of being on the autism spectrum

Some people with AS have a wide range of heightened abilities and sometimes become successful inventors, scientists, musicians and so on.

Exercise 1: Tick the box next to the sentence that describes you the best.

1 I am good at noticing details. ☐

2 I have a good memory for facts or figures. ☐

3 I know a lot about my hobby or interest. ☐

4 I am very honest. ☐

5 I am good at following rules. ☐

6 I like to get on with the job/finish a task. ☐

7 I am a bit of a 'perfectionist' – I like to get things right ☐

8 I can concentrate intensely for long periods ☐

Exercise 2: Describe something you are good at or a special skill or interest you have because you are on the autism spectrum.

....

....

....

....

Exercise 3: Discuss the names and achievements of people who have had AS and have been successful.

For example, Albert Einstein and his theory of relativity

....

....

7 Disclosure

There is no hard-and-fast rule about to whom you should disclose your diagnosis. For some people it is on a 'need-to-know' basis, choosing only to tell selected people. Others tell everybody. One recommended way is by using the 'dripping tap effect' or 'soft disclosure', that is, giving people a little bit of information (a quick summary of the basics) and giving more only if that person is interested and asks about it.

Exercise 1: Who would you tell, or have you told, and why? Describe reactions.

Person/situation	Why might it be good to tell them?	Their reaction

Exercise 2: 'Soft disclosure'. How to disclose information without using a full label? One with poor eye contact could say: 'The reason I'm not looking at you is because I have a sensory integration disorder and find it difficult to look and listen at the same time. I am listening to every word that you say.'

Prepare a sentence of what you might say to people you disclose to as an example of 'soft disclosure.'

....

....

....

....

8 Socialising

Exercise 1: Which social skills do you have a problem with and need to work on improving?

Social skill	Difficulty Yes	No
1 Using eye contact.		
2 Where to stand when talking to people.		
3 How to start a conversation.		
4 Making sure your voice isn't too loud or quiet.		
5 How to show people you're listening to them.		
6 Knowing when you should/shouldn't interrupt.		
7 Not changing the subject too much when talking.		
8 Not talking about your own interests too much.		
9 How to recognise what might upset people.		
10 How to end a conversation.		
11 How to recognise when someone wants to stop talking to you.		

Exercise 2: One way to successfully start a conversation is to think 'what do people talk about?' (WORM). Give an example for something to talk about for each topic.

Weather...

Occupation...

Recreation..

Media..

Exercise 3: What are the pros and cons of small talk? Discuss.

....

....

....

9 Special interests

Many people with AS have special interests and expertise that bring a great deal of pleasure and relaxation.

Exercise 1: For this exercise, find people to work with. Each should list five interests as shown in the table and then discuss them together and with the group.

Person A	Person B
1	1
2	2
3	3
4	4
5	5

Exercise 2: Write down three main reasons why interests can be useful.

1...

2...

3...

Exercise 3: Are there ways your special interest could be used more constructively in your life? Discuss.

....

....

10 Employment

Exercise 1: List your interests and strengths in the first column. Then, in the second column, think about possible jobs that may be relevant to those interests.

Interests/strengths	Possible job

Exercise 2: Identify areas of work where you need support – try to make specific suggestions.

Area where need support	Suggestion

Exercise 3: Identify a problem that has occurred at work before getting your diagnosis and then try to describe in hindsight how you could cope with it better since your diagnosis.

Problem	How you would cope now

11 Getting a balance

A high proportion of people with AS are prone to overstimulation, and then collapse, or have a meltdown, due to an overload of sensory, cognitive or social demands. This needs to be actively managed.

Exercise 1: Think of your resources like a bank account or balance sheet. In the left column, identify things that stress you or 'drain your account'. In the right column, list the things that refresh or 'credit your account'.

Drains	Refreshes
For example, the lights, noise and social demands of a day at work	For example, getting home, being alone and going to bed for half an hour
1	1
2	2
3	3
4	4

Exercise 2: If you have had a 'meltdown' try to understand it using the following terms.

Triggers:..

Thoughts:...

Reaction:..

Exercise 3: Think of a piece of music or an image that describes

How you feel during a meltdown ....

How you are when you are calm ....

12 Empathetic attunement

Empathy is our ability to identify what someone is thinking and feeling and to respond. It has three components: thinking, feeling and behaviour.

Exercise 1: Rate your own empathy. Circle the option that best applies to you.

Thinking: Recognising distress in others	Good	Average	Poor
Feeling: Feeling emotions for others	Good	Average	Poor
Behaviour: Acting compassionately	Good	Average	Poor

Exercise 2: Here are some strategies for improving empathetic attunement. Which statements do you identify with most? Discuss.

1 I say to myself, 'What would another person feel or do in this situation?'

2 I might admit to the person, 'I'm here because I care but I don't know what to do to help.'

3 I have specifically learned about emotions, what they feel like and what situations they occur in.

4 I remind myself to try to think how the other person is feeling, not just myself.

5 I have learned by copying others, watching TV and films and have learned to say things like 'oh dear' and 'Mmm'.

6 I try to be practically helpful and make a cup of tea.

Exercise 3: Identify any ways you have learned to improve your empathic attunement.

....

....

13 Trying to be less rigid, less rule-bound and loosen up

'When I was at work I was always very punctual and never liked being late. However, although this can be viewed as a positive attribute there is also a flip side to it. If somebody was late, I'd find it very difficult to get over my anger, which would often spoil the meeting. I'd think that it was rude and disrespectful.'

Exercise 1: How would you advise somebody trying to overcome the problem mentioned? What could they do, or how could they behave differently? What thoughts could they challenge and attempt to reconstrue to think differently?

....

....

....

....

Exercise 2: Which of these strategies to loosen up your rigid behaviour can you identify with?

- I try to distract myself by doing something different.
- I try to ignore it and make excuses for them.
- I try to replace the word 'should' with 'it would be nice if...'
- I tell the person it really upsets me.
- It eats away at me because they must be thinking, 'my time is more important than your time', which is rude.
- Add your own strategy.

....

....

....

....

14 Advice for somebody who has just received a diagnosis of AS

Exercise 1: What advice would you give to someone who has just received a diagnosis of AS? Read the suggestions and rate how helpful you think these suggestions would be (3 = very helpful; 2 = helpful; 1 = not helpful).

1 Read as much as possible about it. ☐
2 Join a post-diagnostic support group. ☐
3 Expect emotional ups and downs. ☐
4 Join an internet site or forum. ☐
5 Keep a journal or diary, noting changes and making connections. ☐
6 Carry an 'autism alert' card, just in case. ☐
7 Try to spend time with supportive professionals or clinicians. ☐
8 Be careful about disclosure. ☐
9 Attend training workshops and conferences on AS. ☐
10 Be aware that some people, even professionals, don't understand autism. ☐

Exercise 2: What advice would you give to somebody who has just had a diagnosis and what have you found helpful?

....

....

....

Exercise 3: The way forward. Identify two personal goals for the next year, which are specific tasks in which you will attempt to improve the quality of your life following your diagnosis.

....

....

....

Appendix 2

Glossary

Understanding medical and technical terms

Affective empathy	Feeling moved by other people's suffering.
Alexithymia	A condition where an individual struggles to find words for their emotions.
Amygdala	A part of the brain associated with emotions.
Asperger's syndrome (AS)	A milder form of autism, characterised by difficulty with social interaction and narrow interests
Aspie	A colloquial term for someone who has AS.
Attention deficit hyperactivity disorder (ADHD)	A set of behavioural symptoms that include difficulties with attention, hyperactivity and impulsiveness.
Autistic spectrum disorder (ASD)	A term used to describe all the variations of autism. A condition characterised by difficulties with social interaction, communication and behaviour.
Bipolar disorder	A mental health condition, characterised by alternating periods of mania and depression.

Borderline personality disorder (BPD)	A type of personality characterised by difficulty forming and keeping stable relationships, impulsivity and shifting moods.
Cerebellum	A part of the brain located at the back of the head involved in the control of movement, balance and motor coordination.
Clinical psychologist	The branch of psychology dealing with diagnosis and treatment of mental health conditions.
Cognition	The mental process of thought based on knowledge and understanding.
Cognitive behavioural therapy (CBT)	A common therapy to treat conditions like anxiety and depression that aims to help teach people how to manage emotions by changing the way they think and feel.
Co-morbidities	Mental health conditions that occur simultaneously.
Comic strip conversations	Simple drawings such as 'stick figures', with thought and speech bubbles to illustrate the sequence of actions, emotions and thoughts. Originally developed by Carol Gray.

DSM-5	*The Diagnostic and Statistical Manual of Mental Disorders:* 5th Edition.
Dyscalculia	Difficulty understanding even basic mathematical concepts.
Dyslexia	A specific learning difficulty affecting the ability to read and spell.
Dyspraxia	A developmental condition characterised by difficulty involving coordination and movement and planning and organising.
Epilepsy	A neurological condition associated with abnormal electrical activities in the brain resulting in episodes of sensory disturbance and loss of consciousness.
Executive functioning	Skills located in the frontal lobes of the brain involved in planning and organising, multitasking and problem solving.
Fusiform gyrus	An area found in the temporal lobe of the brain, thought to be important in facial recognition, colour processing and word recognition.
Hyperlexia	An advanced ability at reading and recognising words, without prior training and comprehension of the words–a 'superability'.

Hypersensitive	Oversensitive.
Hyposensitive	Undersensitive.
ICD-10	*The International Statistical Classification of Diseases and Related Health Problems* – 10th Edition.
Incidence	The actual number of people with a confirmed diagnosis.
Insula	Area of the brain that receives signals from organs of the body and forms a map of sensation.
Interoception	The ability to detect and attend to bodily sensations.
Learning disability (LD)	A condition associated with learning difficulties, reduced intellectual ability and difficulty with everyday activities.
Monotropism	Restricted interests. Can only pay attention to what is in his or her attention tunnel.
Neurotypical	A term used to describe non-autistic people and their thinking style.
Obsessive compulsive disorder (OCD)	An anxiety disorder associated with obsessions and compulsions.

Olfactory	Sense of smell.
Pedantic speech	Overly formal speech.
Personality disorder	A condition associated with difficulties with relationships and functioning in society.
Pragmatic aspects of language	The modification and use of language in a social context.
Prevalence	The number of people in the general population who have the condition.
Proprioception	The unconscious perception of movement and spatial orientation of the body, limbs and head.
Prosody	The vocal tone and quality of speech.
Prosopagnosia	Face blindness.
Psychiatrist	A medical practitioner specialising in the diagnosis and treatment of mental health conditions.
Psychosis	A mental health condition associated with symptoms such as delusions or hallucinations that suggest impaired contact with reality.
Purkinje cells	Nerve cells, found in the cerebellum, involved with motor coordination.

Schizophrenia	Mental health condition characterised by withdrawal from reality, illogical patterns of thinking, delusions, behaviours and psychotic behaviour.
Semantic pragmatic language disorder (SPLD)	Good language skills in certain areas, such as syntax, vocabulary and phonology, but poor ability of language use in a social context.
Sensory sensitivities	Sensitivity with processing sensory information, such as sound, sight, smell and touch information.
Stimming	Self-stimulating behaviour (flapping hands, licking, spinning, rocking) designed to calm or de-stress.
Synaesthesia	A rare form of sensory perception where two or more sensory experiences are linked (eg colour-number).
Temporal lobe	An area of the brain involved with among other things sound perception, speech, language and memory.
Theory of mind (ToM)	The ability to recognise and understand other people's thoughts, feelings and intentions to understand their behaviour.

Tics	Occasional, involuntary movements or sounds.
Tourette's syndrome	A neurological condition, characterised by involuntary tics and vocalisations.
Weak central coherence	Difficulty understanding the overall picture of something and instead focusing on parts.

Appendix 3

Useful contacts

List of organisations and websites supporting people with AS and their families in the UK

The Autistic Research Centre (ARC)

Part of the University of Cambridge, ARC provides useful information on AS as well as current, relevant research literature on the condition.

For further information: Website: www.autismresearchcentre.com

Asperger's United

A newsletter written for adolescents and adults with AS. Published four times a year.

For more information: National Autistic Society
Tel: +44 (0)20 7903 3542
Website: www.autis.org.uk/aspergerunited

The National Autistic Society (NAS)

393 City Road
London EC1V 1NG
Tel: +44 (0) 20 7833 2299
Helpline: 08450 704 004
Email: nas@nas.org.uk
Website: www.autism.org.uk

Tony Attwood

A guide for individuals with AS, parents and professionals, includes resources, research articles, issues relating to AS and similar topics.

For more information: Website: www.tonyattwood.com.au

Wrong Planet

A web community designed for individuals (as well as their families and professionals) with AS and other neurological difficulties. The website has discussion forums, where members can communicate with one another online, interesting articles to read, how-to-guides and blogs.

For more information: Website: www.wrongplanet.net

Appendix 4

List of useful books for further reading

Asperger H (1944) 'Autistic psychopathy in childhood', Frith U (ed), *Autism and Asperger Syndrome*, Cambridge University Press, Cambridge.

Aston M (2009) *The Asperger Couples Workbook*, Jessica Kingsley Publications, London.

Attwood T (2008) *The Complete Guide to Asperger's Syndrome*, Jessica Kingsley Publications, London.

Attwood T (ed) (2014) *Been There, Done That, Try This! An Aspie Guide to Life on Earth*, Jessica Kingsley Publications, London.

Baron-Cohen S (2008) *Autism and Asperger Syndrome*, Oxford University Press, Oxford.

Baron-Cohen S (2011) *Zero Degrees of Empathy*, Allen Lane, London.

The Diagnostic and Statistical Manual of Mental Disorders: 5th Edition (2013) American Psychiatric Association, Washington, DC.

Don van J & Zucker C (2016) *In a Different Key: The Story of Autism*, Allen Lane, London.

Grandin T (2006) *Thinking in Pictures*, Bloomsbury Publishing, London.

Grandin T & Panek R (2013) *The Autistic Brain*, Rider, Ebury Publishing, London.

Jackson L (2002) *Freaks, Geeks and Asperger Syndrome*, Jessica Kingsley Publications, London.

Ledgin N (2002). *Asperger's and Self-Esteem*, Future Horizons, Texas.

Murray D (ed) (2006) *Coming Out Asperger*, Jessica Kingsley Publications, London.

Ramachandran VS (2011) *The Tell-Tale Brain*, William Heinemann, London.

Santomauro J (ed) (2012) *Autism All-Stars*, Jessica Kingsley Publications, London.

Silberman S (2015) *Neurotribes*, Allen & Unwin, London.

Stanford A (2011) *Business for Aspies*, Jessica Kingsley Publications, London.

Willey LH (1999) *Pretending to Be Normal: Living with Asperger's Syndrome*, Jessica Kingsley Publications, London.

Williams D (1992) *Nobody, Nowhere*, Time Books, New York.

Wylie P (2015) *Very late Diagnosis of Asperger Syndrome (Autism Spectrum Disorder)*, Jessica Kingsley Publications, London.

Appendix 5

The adult autism spectrum quotient (AQ)

Reproduced with kind permission from the Autism Research Unit University of Cambridge. For full details, see S Baron-Cohen, S Wheelwright, R Skinner, J Martin and E Clubley (2001) 'The Autism Spectrum Quotient (AQ): evidence from Asperger Syndrome/ High Functioning Autism, males and females, scientists and mathematicians,' *Journal of Autism and Developmental Disorders* 31, pp5–17. This is downloadable from http://autismresearchcentre.com. This is a screening and research tool, not a direct diagnostic tool.

The AQ is provided for research use only and should not be used to inform clinical decisions. Any commercial use of the AQ is prohibited without prior express written permission from the creators and the Autism Research Centre at the University of Cambridge.

Responses that score 1 point are marked. Other responses score 0. For total score, sum all item

		Definitely agree	**Slightly agree**	**Slightly disagree**	**Definitely disagree**
1	I prefer to do things with others rather than on my own			1	1
2	I prefer to do things the same way over and over again	1	1		
3	If I try to imagine something, I find it easy to create a picture in my mind			1	1
4	I frequently get so strongly absorbed in one thing that I lose sight of other things	1	1		

		Definitely agree	Slightly agree	Slightly disagree	Definitely disagree
5	I often notice small sounds when others do not	1	1		
6	I usually notice car number plates or similar things of information	1	1		
7	Other people frequently tell me that what I've said is impolite, even though I think it is polite	1	1		
8	When I'm reading a story, I can easily imagine what the characters might look like			1	1
9	I am fascinated by dates	1	1		
10	In a social group, I can easily keep track of several different people's conversations			1	1
11	I find social situations easy			1	1
12	I tend to notice details that others do not	1	1		
13	I would rather go to a library than go to a party	1	1		
14	I find making up stories easy			1	1
15	I find myself drawn more strongly to people than things			1	1
16	I tend to have very strong interests, which I get upset about if I can't pursue	1	1		
17	I enjoy social chit-chat			1	1

(*continued*)

(*continued*)

		Definitely agree	Slightly agree	Slightly disagree	Definitely disagree
18	When I talk, it isn't always easy for others to get a word in edgeways	1	1		
19	I am fascinated by numbers	1	1		
20	When I'm reading a story, I find it difficult to work out the characters' intentions	1	1		
21	I don't particularly enjoy reading fiction	1	1		
22	I find it hard to make new friends	1	1		
23	I notice patterns in things all the time	1	1		
24	I would rather go to the theatre than to a museum			1	1
25	It does not upset me if my daily routine is disturbed			1	1
26	I frequently find that I don't know how to keep a conversation going	1	1		
27	I find it easy to 'read between the lines' when someone is talking to me			1	1
28	I usually concentrate more on the whole picture, rather than on the small details			1	1
29	I am not very good at remembering phone numbers			1	1
30	I don't usually notice small changes in a situation, or a person's appearance			1	1

		Definitely agree	**Slightly agree**	**Slightly disagree**	**Definitely disagree**
31	I know how to tell if someone listening to me is getting bored			1	1
32	I find it easy to do more than one thing at once			1	1
33	When I talk on the phone, I'm not sure when it's my turn to speak	1	1		
34	I enjoy doing things spontaneously			1	1
35	I am often the last to understand the point of a joke	1	1		
36	I find it easy to work out what someone is thinking or feeling just by looking at their face			1	1
37	If there is an interruption, I can switch to what I was doing very quickly			1	1
38	I am good at social chit-chat			1	1
39	People often tell me that I keep going on and on about the same thing	1	1		
40	When I was young, I used to enjoy playing games involving pretending with other children			1	1
41	I like to collect information about categories of things (eg types of cars, birds, trains, plants)	1	1		

(*continued*)

		Definitely agree	**Slightly agree**	**Slightly disagree**	**Definitely disagree**
42	I find it difficult to imagine what it would be like to be someone else	1	1		
43	I like to carefully plan any activities I participate in	1	1		
44	I enjoy social occasions			1	1
45	I find it difficult to work out people's intentions	1	1		
46	New situations make me anxious	1	1		
47	I enjoy meeting new people			1	1
48	I am a good diplomat			1	1
49	I am not very good at remembering people's date of birth			1	1
50	I find it very easy to play games with children that involve pretending			1	1

How to interpret your score?

- 0–10 = Low
- 11–22 = average (most women score around 15 and men score about 17)
- 23–31 = above average
- 32–50 = very high (most people with AS/ASD score about 35)
- 50 = maximum

Answers to the autism quiz on page 000: True: 2, 3, 5, 6, 7, 8, 9; False: 1, 4, 10

References

Baird G, Simonoff E, Pickles A, Chandler S, Loucas T, Meldrum D & Charman T (2006) Prevelance of disorders of autism spectrum in a population cohort of children in South Thames, *Lancet*, July 15; 368(9531): 210–15

Cassidy S, Bradley P, Robinson J, Allison C, McHugh M & Baron-Cohen S (2014) 'Suicidal ideation and suicide plans or attempts in adults with Asperger's syndrome attending a specialist diagnostic clinic: a clinical cohort study', *The Lancet Psychiatry*, 1 (2), pp142–47.

Dalton KM, Nacewicz BM, Johnson T, Schaeper HS, Gernbacher MA, Goldsmith HHJH, Alexander AL & Davidson EJ (2005) 'Gaze fixation and neural circuitry of face processing in autism', *Nature Neurosceience*, 8, pp519–26.

Howlin P, Goode S, Hutton J & Rutter M (2004) 'Adult outcomes for children with autism', *Journal Of Child Psychology and Psychiatry*, 45, pp212–29.

King MD, Fountain C, Dakhallah D & Bearman P (2008) 'Estimated autism risk and older reproductive age', *American Journal of Public Health*, 99 (9), pp1673–79.

Kolevzon A, Gross R & Reichberg A (2007) 'Prenatal and perinatal risk factors for autism', *Arch Pediatric Adolescent Medicine*, 161 (4), pp326–33.

Seitzer M, Kraus M, Shatluck P, Orsmond G, Swe A & Lord C (2003) 'The symptoms of autism spectrum disorders in adolescence and adulthood', *Journal of Autism and Developmental Disorders*, 33 (6), pp565–81.

Smith Myles B, Tapsco H, Cook K, Miller N, Rinner L & Robbins L (2000) *Asperger Syndrome & Sensory Issues*, Autism, Asperger Publishing Company, Shawnee Mission, KS.

Synder A, Ellwood S & Chi R (2012) 'Switching on creativity', *Scientific American Mind*, 22, pp58–62.

Treasure J (2013) 'Coherence and other autistic spectrum traits and eating disorders', *Nordic Journal of Psychiatry*, 67 (1), pp38–42.

Volkmar F, Klin A & Pauls D (1998) 'Nosologial and genetic aspects of Asperger syndrome', *Journal of Autism & Developmental Disorders*, 28, pp457–63.